THE ROYAL HOSPITAL CHELSEA
THE PLACE AND THE PEOPLE

THE ROYAL HOSPITAL CHELSEA

THE PLACE AND THE PEOPLE

THIRD MILLENNIUM
PUBLISHING, LONDON

First published in 2004 by Third Millennium Publishing Limited,
a subsidiary of Third Millennium Information Limited
Farringdon House
2nd Floor
105–107 Farringdon Road
London
EC1R 3BU
www.tmiltd.com

ISBN: 1 903942 27 6

Project Editor: Elizabeth Drury
Designer: Helen Swansbourne, London
Picture Researcher: Philippa Lewis

Produced by Third Millennium Publishing Limited, a subsidiary of
Third Millennium Information Limited
Printed and bound in Slovenia by Mladinska

Endpapers: 'South East View of Chelsea Hospital', aquatint after
Lynn, published in 1818; 'The Grand Fancy Fair, Chelsea College
Gardens', lithograph of *c.* 1842.
Frontispiece: View through Wren's portico and along the colonnade
of the south front.

CONTENTS

ACKNOWLEDGEMENTS

This book was the idea, way back in 2000, of the Lieutenant-Governor of the Royal Hospital, Major General Jonathan Hall CBE OBE who, with Liz Drury, succeeded in getting the project off the ground. Once the Commissioners of the Royal Hospital had given their wholehearted support, planning started immediately. Among those who have been instrumental in ensuring that it became a reality were Julian Platt of Third Millennium Publishing and Major John Tatham, Curator at the Royal Hospital. Grateful thanks are due also to Christopher Pocock and the Belgravia Traders' Association, whose members – listed on page 186 – raised considerable sums in support of the project, and to the individual subscribers to the book whose names appear on that page; also to Ronald Gerard OBE, a notable benefactor of the Royal Hospital, for his substantial contribution towards the cost of the new photography.

AUTHOR'S ACKNOWLEDGEMENTS

I would like to thank the following people for their special help with the research, writing and production of this book: In-Pensioner Martin Ford for his many useful insights and suggestions about the history of the Royal Hospital; also In-Pensioners Alfred Amphlett BEM, Charles Boyce DCM, Frank Chambers, Ralph Dickinson, William Germanes, Charlie Hackney, Archibald Harrington OBE, John Jones, William Moylon, Buck Taylor, Tom Parnell, Geoffrey Payne and all the other In-Pensioners who were kind enough to share their memories with me. Thanks also to Jon Nuttall for his help in understanding the history and often mysterious workings of the Royal Hospital, Major John Tatham for his good humour and tireless efforts to introduce me to, and make available, the vast repository of material on the history of the Royal Hospital, Liz Drury for her hard work in preparing the text for publication, for checking facts and for spotting unfortunate omissions, Pippa Lewis for her discovery and selection of appropriate and very fine images of the Royal Hospital and Chelsea and members of the Royal Hospital staff who contributed in so many ways; and last, King Charles II, Sir Christopher Wren and Sir Stephen Fox for giving London one of its greatest and most worthwhile institutions and to the craftsmen who realized that vision in such memorable form.

OPPOSITE: *Detail from the overmantel in the Council Chamber carved by William Emmett.*

CALENDAR NOTE

The calendar introduced on the Continent by Pope Gregory XIII in 1582 was accepted in Britain in 1752. With the Gregorian calendar the new year begins on 1 January rather than on 25 March, the Feast of the Annunciation, as previously. The dates given here for the days between January and March are in this 'new style': thus, on page 58, the Royal Warrant is dated January 1691, which by modern reckoning would be 1692.

I believe that for both Londoners and visitors alike, one of the most evocative moments in our capital city is to glimpse one of the 350 or so "Chelsea Pensioners", nattily attired in their scarlet- or navy-blue-clad coats, parading down the King's Road from their home at The Royal Hospital.

For more than three hundred years the great building by the Thames has been a place of refuge for some of our proud veterans from the British Army. It was in December 1681 that King Charles II issued a Warrant for the construction of a building "for the succour and relief of Veterans broken by Age and War". That The Royal Hospital continues to care for the retired soldiers, and to impress the passer-by, is – it seems to me – a tribute to the particular talents of two men: Sir Stephen Fox, who helped the King to finance the enterprise, and Sir Christopher Wren, who designed and supervised the construction of the building.

But we must pay tribute, too, to the other great architects and craftsmen who played their part in creating what we see today – William Cleere and Sir Charles Hopson, who were Wren's joiners; John Grove and Henry Margetts, his plasterers; William Emmett and William Morgan, his carvers; Robert Adam, who undertook some minor alterations; and Sir John Soane, some sympathetic development. Grinling Gibbons carved the marvellous statue of the Hospital's Founder, and the painting by Sebastiano Ricci and his nephew Marco of *Christ Rising from the Tomb* adorns the apse of the Chapel. The simplicity, grandeur and 'fitness for purpose' of the buildings are, to my mind, perfectly and timelessly blended: it is a group of buildings which I, personally, greatly admire.

But, as the title of this informative and beautifully illustrated book suggests, it is about more than the building. It is about the Chelsea Pensioners – their memories and their humour (despite old age and infirmity) which are very much part of the atmosphere of the place.

Today, as in previous generations, the British soldier stands ready to fight for his country, but now he is as often called upon to serve as a peace-keeper, providing humanitarian aid and internal security, and sometimes to restore order and maintain essential services when the civil authorities are not able to do so. Supporting these Pensioners are the staff. Some continue to bear the names of historic offices and, while keeping alive the old traditions, they care devotedly for those at the Royal Hospital. I have been impressed by their constant striving to keep the Hospital up-to-date and congratulate them and the Board of Commissioners on the exciting plans that are being made to give the Royal Hospital a secure future.

Our soldiers are as deserving of shelter and care in retirement as they were when the Hospital was founded. As Patron of the Royal Hospital Appeal, I am delighted to commend this inspiring story of a great institution - a symbol of the Nation's gratitude to veterans of the Army.

William Moylon

WILLIAM MOYLON HAD JOINED THE ROYAL IRISH FUSILIERS IN June 1940, was posted to the 6th Battalion the Royal Inniskilling Fusiliers in February 1941 and his war started in earnest in February 1942 when he found himself crammed aboard an antique and ailing troopship – the *Empress of Asia* – on his way to strengthen the British garrison at Singapore. 'It was a "hell-ship",' remembers Moylon, 'bad food, terrible sanitation and we had no idea where we were going.' Then, twenty miles from their destination, the ship was attacked by Japanese bombers. The first attack disabled the ship, the second sank her: 'five or six bombs hit us and she burnt like paper'.

It was a long jump into the water and this made Moylon's friend Reagan fearful of going over the side. 'I urged him to come, but he wouldn't. I jumped and never saw Reagan again. He was killed.' This was the first of a series of emotional hammer blows. The men in the water had to fight for the few rafts and as they did so were machine-gunned by the Japanese planes. Moylon, battling with a large number of survivors to hang on to a seven-feet-square float, was in the water for four hours before being picked up by an Indian gunboat.

Within ten days of being landed at Singapore he found himself in the midst of one of the greatest tragedies ever to befall British forces. On 15th February 1942 the great city and fortress of Singapore surrendered to the Japanese and Moylon was among thousands of prisoners of war. For the next three years he toiled for the Japanese, initially building prison camps and then on the railway through Thailand, including the famous wooden bridge over the River Kwai. The conditions – and the behaviour of the Japanese – grew appalling. Moylon remembers that things were not too bad at first but, by the end, 'the Japs were terrible, terrible – all they ever said was "speedo"'.

He arrived back in Britain in October 1945 and was discharged from the Army in July 1946. In March 1999, at the age of eighty-two, William Moylon entered the Royal Hospital.

CHELSEA

Albert Edward (Charlie) Hackney

CHARLIE HACKNEY'S EXPERIENCES IN THE ARMY READ like an adventure story. He enlisted in the 15/19th Hussars in 1935 and on arrival in India joined the 13/18th Hussars on the North West Frontier and so started his military career in fine imperial manner. In January 1940 he returned to Europe and went straight to France as part of the British Expeditionary Force. He was based in Arras, saw heavy fighting, and was eventually evacuated from Dunkirk. After recovering from a head wound, Hackney joined the 48th Tank Battalion of the Royal Armoured Corps and soon after volunteered for service with the Army's 5 Commando and with them was involved in the raid on the Lofoten islands, off Norway. Returning to the Royal Armoured Corps, he was trained to operate Crusader tanks and was sent to North Africa to join the 4th Hussars. He managed to lose two tanks in two weeks – through enemy action – and, when the Squadron Sergeant-Major upbraided him for his carelessness and ordered him to find another tank, Hackney's response was colourful. 'I told him to "get stuffed". I didn't like his attitude.'

Hackney was threatened with a court martial, but before anything happened he was rescued by the SAS. He met Major 'Paddy' Mayne who thought it very strange that a man should be punished for losing two tanks in action and, clearly admiring Hackney's independent spirit, invited him to join the SAS. This Hackney did. After 'lying low' in the desert for two months, on patrol with the legendary Long Range Desert Group, he joined 2 SAS under Colonel Bill Stirling and was attached to No 1 Squadron under Major Roy Farran. This unit was tasked to carry out a raid from a submarine, to destroy the lighthouse on Pantelleria, in the Mediterranean. In September 1943 they were part of the force that seized Taranto and the following month were involved in the audacious commando operations that secured the town and port of Termoli.

When the second front opened after Normandy, Hackney and 2 SAS operated in north-west Europe: dropping behind German lines to destroy a convoy of vehicles loaded with some 40,000 gallons of fuel, attacking across the Rhine and involvement in a series of operations on the way to Lüneberg. When the war ended Hackney and 2 SAS were in Norway, but their appetite for action was thwarted by the German surrender that took place while the squadron was flying in from Brussels.

Hackney, a sergeant by the end of the war with the Croix de Guerre, entered the Royal Hospital in 2000, at the age of eighty-two.

Archibald Harrington OBE

ARCHIE HARRINGTON'S CAREER MUST BE UNIQUE IN the annals of the Royal Hospital. He enlisted in the Royal Artillery in November 1924 and by the time the war ended he had received an Emergency Commission, had been Mentioned in Despatches no less than three times between 1942 and 1945 and was an acting lieutenant-colonel on the staff of the 5th Indian Division. In 1946 – by then having received an OBE for his military service – Harrington was made a Regular Army officer.

The first phase of Harrington's military career centred around India, where he was posted in 1934 to police the North West Frontier and show the flag along the Khyber Pass. In April 1940 Harrington – by now a warrant officer, married and a self-taught Urdu speaker with an intimate knowledge of much of India – received an Emergency Commission and was posted to the 5th Indian Division as an Adjutant. 'I am an extremely fortunate man,' admits Harrington, 'life has smiled on me.' The Division was posted to the Sudan and by 1941 was fighting in North Africa where Harrington was in command of an anti-tank battery and an attached infantry unit. Later in the year he was made a staff captain in the Royal Artillery HQ of that division and ended the war in Burma.

Harrington served in the Army for almost twenty-eight years and entered the Royal Hospital in 1997 at the age of ninety. He was eligible because, although ending his military career as an officer, he had served for over twelve years in the ranks. Living on equal terms with In-Pensioners whom he could have commanded, and could have had disciplinary power over, has not proved difficult for him. 'I am a soldier – pure and simple – like the other men here. I don't boast about my rank. It rebounds to your credit if you don't talk about it. Inside here I'm a former NCO. When I go outside, I'm a former lieutenant-colonel.'

PENSIONERS

Charles Boyce DCM

CHARLIE BOYCE JOINED THE 2ND BATTALION THE Monmouthshire Regiment in April 1940 but it was not until July 1944 – going into Normandy over a month after the invasion – that he first saw action. From then until the end of the war Boyce found himself pretty well in the thick of things.

When he landed in Normandy, Boyce was a sergeant in a battery of towed 6-pounder anti-tank guns that were part of 53rd Reconnaissance Regiment. The 6-pounder was, remembers Boyce, 'a wonderful gun' and on two occasions, using armour-piercing rounds with steel cores, Boyce managed to knock out two German tanks – and survive.

Boyce was in the Ardennes in December 1944, during the Battle of the Bulge, when the Germans launched their final desperate counter-attack with a view to gaining victory over the Allied armies. What he remembers best is the appalling cold.

In April 1945 – just as the war was about to end – Boyce suddenly found himself in a most perilous situation. His troop had been ordered to seize the bridge at Kluverborstel, near Bremen. As they approached, the British troops came under fire from German machine guns and mortars. The British armoured cars returned fire and Boyce deployed his two guns and started firing high-explosive shells at the German positions across the river.

Suddenly two of the men on one of Boyce's guns were wounded. It was a critical moment – Boyce had to call up replacements to keep the gun in action – and it fell to him to rescue and treat his two men while under enemy fire. 'I pushed Private Boniface with my head – my helmet and nose almost on the ground – into the safety of a nearby ditch. And then I had to get Corporal Moffatt who kept crying out "leave me! leave me!" because of the enemy fire, but I got him into cover as well. The wounded men had to be got to the rear for treatment – both had broken legs. As the enemy fire was so intense a lance-corporal refused my orders to leave the ditch to escort the wounded back, so I took the men back myself. It was an awkward thing to do – to leave my command under fire – it's what you should never do. But I had to get them back and I couldn't let the driver and wounded go back unescorted.' For his actions during the capture of the bridge Charles Boyce was awarded an immediate Distinguished Conduct Medal. He entered the Royal Hospital in 2002 at the age of eighty-six.

INTRODUCTION

BY

THE GOVERNOR OF THE ROYAL HOSPITAL
GENERAL SIR JEREMY MACKENZIE GCB OBE

THE ROYAL HOSPITAL CHELSEA was founded to provide accommodation and care for veterans of the British Army and this it has done throughout its long history. Links with the past are strong. On Founder's Day the Chelsea Pensioners celebrate the birthday of their benefactor, Charles II, and the anniversary of his accession and the restoration of the monarchy in May 1660.

But it is, as well, a living place, providing the Pensioners with comfortable board and lodging, a convivial environment and a variety of opportunities for self-fulfilment through mental and physical recreation. In addition, its medical and nursing facilities are second to none. When the Pensioners are sick or in need of nursing, they are looked after in the Royal Hospital's own Infirmary.

At the heart of life at the Royal Hospital is the building designed by Sir Christopher Wren. Thomas Carlyle, the nineteenth-century historian and resident of Chelsea, wrote: 'I had passed it almost daily for many years without thinking much about it, and I looked at it more attentively, and I saw that it was quiet and dignified, and the work of a gentleman'. In its quiet dignity, the Royal Hospital is a masterpiece of British architecture.

Pensioners still sleep in Wren's Long Wards and eat in his Great Hall. They attend services in his Chapel and take their ease on seats under the loggia designed by him. No institution can stand still, though, and plans are being prepared that will enable the Royal Hospital to meet modern standards by building a new Infirmary and improving living conditions in the Long Wards.

The Pensioners are familiar and popular figures in and around Chelsea, and in the many parts of the world, such as the United States of America and the Far East, to which groups of them have travelled. Wherever they are, their distinctive uniform signifies loyalty to the Sovereign and to their country.

The accounts of Pensioners of the twenty-first century, of their experiences during their years of service in the British Army and in retirement, bring the Chelsea story up to date. They illustrate the continuing importance of providing a refuge for them in old age, and the companionship and care that the Royal Hospital has offered from the very beginning.

I
THE FOUNDATION OF
THE ROYAL HOSPITAL

OPPOSITE: *Charles II in the dress of a Roman general. The statue was commissioned from Grinling Gibbons and presented to the King by Tobias Rustat, one of the original benefactors of the Hospital. The sculpture was regilded to commemorate Queen Elizabeth II's Golden Jubilee in 2002.*

ABOVE: *Charles I and his family, a picture acquired for the Governor's Parlour, now the Council Chamber, by 1700. It is a version of the painting by Sir Anthony Van Dyck in the Royal Collection and it shows the future Charles II standing by his father and the future James II on the knee of his mother, Queen Henrietta Maria.*

PREVIOUS PAGE: *Painting of Figure Court by Dirk Maes, 1717, with the statue of Charles II, founder of the Royal Hospital, in the foreground. The Hospital is a monumental building with a domestic character and it enshrines the spirit of English architecture.*

IN FEBRUARY 1692 the first of the Chelsea Pensioners were admitted to the Royal Hospital in Chelsea. It was a little more than ten years since King Charles II had declared his intention of founding a hospital 'for the relief of such Land Souldiers as are, or shall be, old, lame, or infirme in ye Service of the Crowne'. Since that time James II had briefly occupied the throne and the Crown was now held jointly by his daughter Mary and her husband William III.

The forces behind the creation of the Royal Hospital were complex and the men involved in its foundation among the most powerful in the land. They were part of the Stuart establishment and able in many fields: politics, science and the arts – a heady combination indeed.

The story of the Royal Hospital properly begins in the 1670s, an uncertain time for the Stuart monarchy with the country far from stable and confident of a secure future. The fighting of the Civil War was less than thirty years distant and Charles II had regained the throne in 1660 in most curious circumstances. He was invited back – from the protection of foreign courts – by the very men who had defeated his father and forced the young prince into dangerous exile. But the monarchy that Charles regained was very different from that which his father had finally lost in 1648.

Charles I ruled by Divine Right, as God's anointed on earth. Charles II ruled as a constitutional monarch – as a figurehead appointed and controlled politically by the men who brought him back – by Parliament which was, in a limited way, elected by and representative of the people. So the King, in a sense, ruled by the agreement of his people. They – not he – held the real power in the land. At any time he could – in theory – be dismissed.

In 1661, in this precarious situation, Charles had established for the first time in British history a standing – regular – army. It was small – only around 7,000 men – but many people found the idea distinctly troubling. Why, they asked, did a monarch have need of such a force in peacetime unless he had a plan to overthrow Parliament and set himself up as a despot. Veterans from Charles's army would add to the demand by old and invalid soldiers for financial and material support.

Provision for the upkeep of army veterans had been in existence for many years but was not always satisfactory. In 1593 Parliament had passed a statute for the relief of

VIRTUTI
BELLICÆ

soldiers who had 'adventured their lives or lost their limbs in the service of Her Majesty and the State'. To gain this relief soldiers had to apply to the treasurer of the county in which they were born or where they had lived for at least three years with a certificate from their chief commander or captain giving particulars of their hurts and service record. The maximum pension was £10 a year for a soldier and £20 for an officer.

This legislation – limited as it was – carried a painful sting calculated to appeal to civilian authorities. Any pensioned soldier who was caught begging was to be punished as a 'common rogue' and lose his pension. So this act was essentially part of the Poor Law and anti-vagrancy legislation.

The Statute for Maimed Soldiers lapsed at the outbreak of the Civil War but in March 1643 Parliament ordered collections to be made in each parish and established hospitals in London – such as the Savoy – and wards in St Bartholomew's and St Thomas's hospitals for wounded soldiers with nurses selected from among soldiers' widows. In 1646 the London town house of the Bishop of Ely was fitted up as a military hospital to provide additional accommodation. By 1654 a Parliamentary Committee reported that about 6,000 army pensioners and dependants were being maintained at an expense of just over £40,000 a year.

The restoration of the monarchy created a series of interesting problems. Fearful former Parliamentary soldiers petitioned for their existing allowances to be continued. Instead the Statute for Maimed Soldiers was re-established and it was ordered that the existing pensioners should be provided for under its – less indulgent – conditions. By September 1660 both the Savoy and Ely House had been closed.

Maimed or destitute Royalist soldiers posed an additional problem because many of them had been financially ruined through their support of the royal cause and for the previous ten years had lived in poverty. In an attempt to compensate this class of military veteran Parliament voted them grants and, in 1662, the Statute for Maimed Soldiers was extended to cover destitute Royalist, as well as maimed, soldiers.

But money was in short supply and corruption and incompetence rife, so many of the Civil War veterans who were eligible for relief simply did not get the pensions due to them. The profits from lotteries organized by the King in London in 1668 were casually embezzled by the lottery trustees.

LEFT: *Kilmainham Hospital, near Dublin, built for superannuated soldiers of the Irish Army and based on the idea of the Hôtel des Invalides. It was designed by Sir William Robinson and the foundation stone was laid in 1680; the first veterans arrived in March 1684.*

In 1672 Charles's eldest illegitimate son, the Duke of Monmouth, visited Paris and while there he inspected the works at the Hôtel des Invalides. Begun in 1670 on the orders of Louis XIV, the hospital was intended to house 5,000 old soldiers and – as befitted the autocratic court of the French King – it was also intended to hold its place in Paris as a great public building and celebrate French military triumph.

The Invalides offered an intriguing solution. If Charles were to build a similar establishment in London it would solve the pressing problem of housing the old soldiers with dignity, and in the process create a handsome architectural ornament to his reign. As a conspicuous act of benevolence it would encourage enlistment in his army and promote loyalty to the King among his soldiers. Ultimately it might act as a barracks

BELOW: *Royal arms from the dining room at Kilmainham, now displayed in the Octagon Porch of the Royal Hospital.*

S^R STEPHEN FOX
DIED 1716.

LEFT: *Sir Stephen Fox (1627–1716), a portrait by John James Bakker. Fox was charged by Charles II with finding a way of financing the Royal Hospital and was the guiding hand during the early years. At his funeral it was said that his reason for devoting time and his own money to the Hospital was that 'he could not bear to see the common souldiers who had spent their strength in our service, to beg at our doors'.*

in central London for a veteran, armed and loyal royal bodyguard. The creation of the Royal Hospital could in part be seen as an aspect of a deep-laid plan for his own survival.

In 1677 Monmouth returned to Paris, visited the Invalides again – which had started to receive army veterans the previous year – and wrote to the Marquis de Louvois, the French Minister of War, asking for plans of the building. There was, it seems, no response, but by then the concept had already been imitated in Ireland.

In 1675 the creation of a similar hospital for veterans of the Irish Army was suggested by the Lord-Lieutenant of Ireland, the Duke of Ormonde. Such an institution would relieve the Army of responsibility for men who were no longer fit for active military duties. The building would be located at Kilmainham just outside Dublin and house 300 pensioners. It was to cost £23,000 and the budget was submitted to the Treasury in England for approval in April 1679. The proposal was accepted and three months

ABOVE: *Coat of arms of Sir Stephen Fox and dedication to him, as one of the Lords Commissioners of His Majesty's Treasury and Commissioner of the Royal Hospital, from the engraving by Richard Inglish reproduced on pages 24–25.*

LEFT: *'King James's College at Chelsea' as it should have looked. Chelsea College was a theological college founded by James I to counter 'the pedantry, sophistry, and novelties of the Jesuits, and other [of] the Pope's factors and followers'. The building was used to house prisoners of war and in 1667, still uncompleted and in a partly ruinous state, it was given by Charles II to the Royal Society. In 1682 Fox paid £1,300 for the Chelsea site for the Royal Hospital.*

BELOW: *Dedication to Sir Christopher Wren, as Surveyor of His Majesty's Works and Commissioner of the Royal Hospital, from the engraving by Inglish reproduced on pages 24–25.*

later was approved by the King. Work on the building, designed in a modest but noble manner by Sir William Robinson, the Surveyor-General, started in 1680 and in 1684 the Hospital received its first pensioners. (It operated as originally intended until 1923 and is now a museum.)

Kilmainham was built and financed by a system of poundage on pay. The sum of 6d. in the pound was deducted from the pay of all ranks in the Irish Army and so it was that serving soldiers paid for the hospital for old soldiers.

In early September 1681 the Earl of Longford – who had laid the foundation stone at Kilmainham the previous year and was a member of its Standing Committee – arrived from Ireland and had a number of audiences with the King. How to apply the lessons of Kilmainham to a London establishment must have been the topic. It would seem that Charles was confident that the problem had been solved in principle for on 6th September he referred Longford to the Treasury to talk over the mechanics of the proposal.

Less than two weeks later the project had become tangible. The King had evidently instructed Sir Stephen Fox to deal with the setting up of an English equivalent to Kilmainham. Indeed the diarist John Evelyn, a member of the Royal Society, recorded on 14th September that he had dined with Fox,

> who propos'd to me the purchasing of Chelsey College, which his Majesty had some time since given to our Society, and would now purchase it againe to build an Hospital or Infirmary for Souldiers there, in which he desired my assistance as one of the Council of the Royal Society.

Chelsea College had been the idea of Matthew Sutcliffe, Dean of Exeter, and King James I and was intended for the study of theology. It was part of James's plan to

ABOVE: *Sir Christopher Wren (1632–1723),
Edmund Dyer's copy at the Royal Hospital of
the portrait by Sir Godfrey Kneller.
Mathematician, astronomer, anatomist and*
*architect, President of the Royal Society and
Surveyor of the King's Works, Wren was one of
the most brilliant men of his age. The
foundation of the Royal Hospital was greatly*
*owing to him. Not only did he design the
building but, according to his grandson, he
compiled the statutes and settled the whole
'oeconomy of the House'.*

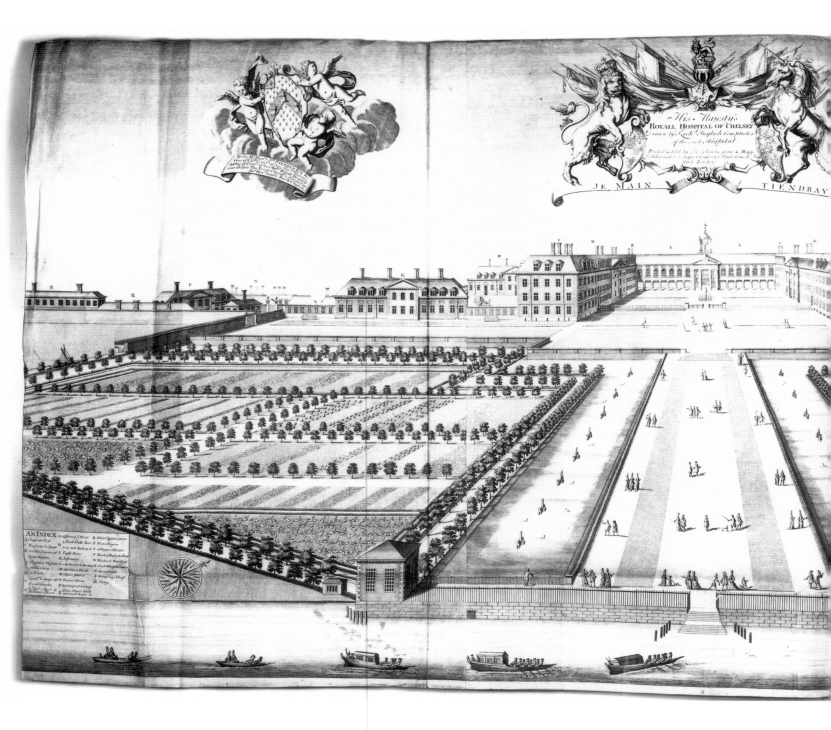

encourage a Protestant riposte to the Counter-Reformation doctrines emanating from Rome. It was not a success and its pair of quadrangles (built by 1618 and sited where the south-west wing of the Royal Hospital now stands) were acquired by the Government in 1660 to house Dutch and Scottish prisoners of war. In 1666 the dilapidated and antiquated buildings had been granted by the Crown to the newly created Royal Society.

The Royal Society for the Improvement of Natural Knowledge was a scholarly

ABOVE: 'His Majesty's Royal Hospital at Chelsey', c. 1700, from a drawing by Richard Inglish, printed and sold by Thomas Bowles. The engraving shows Wren's original court flanked by the two wings of Pensioners' accommodation. To the left is the original Infirmary

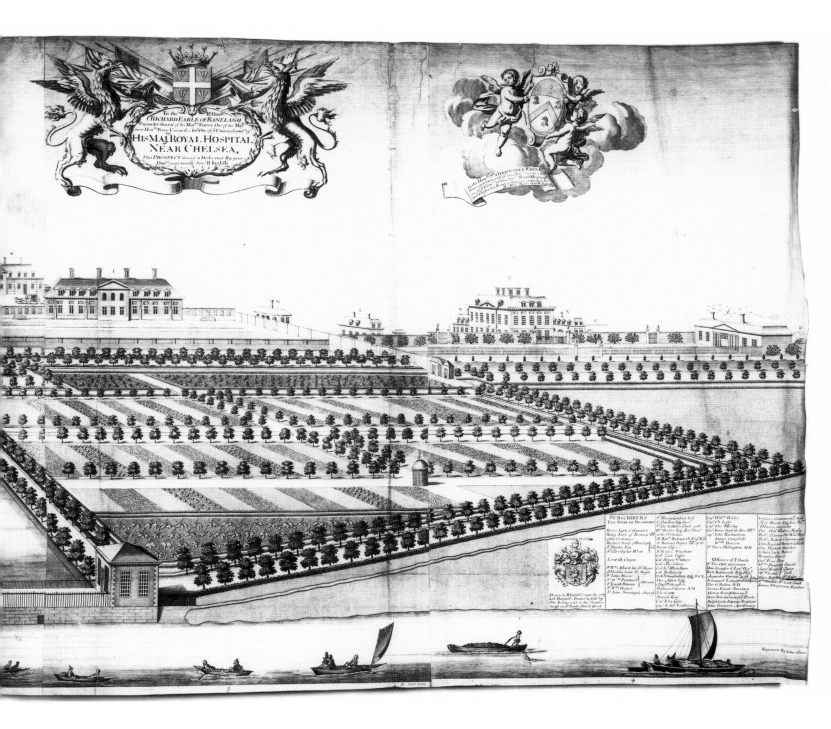

and to the right Light Horse Court. It shows also the elevated central causeway and canals stretching down to the river. The large building on the right is Ranelagh House.

and enterprising creation and one in which the King himself became very closely involved. It was granted the first of its Royal Charters in 1662 and Sir Christopher Wren was a founding member of Council. In January 1681 he became President.

Wren was trying to dispose of the Chelsea site which, with its now-ruinous buildings, was of no use to the Royal Society. In October 1681 Wren told the Council that he, with Evelyn, was negotiating with Sir Stephen Fox for the sale of all the Society's Chelsea possessions. The asking price was £1,500.

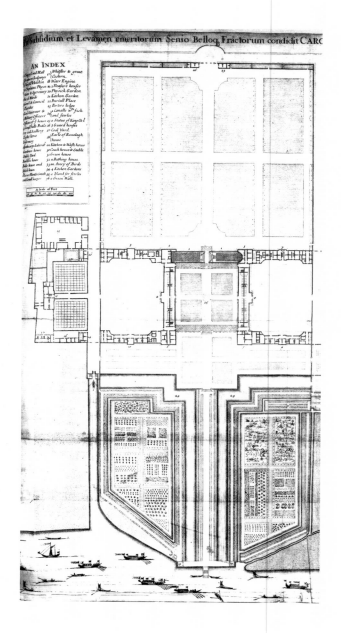

LEFT: *Detail of a general plan of the Royal Hospital engraved by Robert Inglish in 1691 from a drawing probably by Nicholas Hawksmoor. It shows the two courts that were added for James II on either side of Figure Court – Infirmary (now College) Court to the west and Light Horse Court to the east – and the group of buildings to the west that included the Bake House, the Wash House and the quarters of the Whitster, who was responsible for the laundry.*

BELOW: *Dedication of the plan to Lord Ranelagh.*

Fox was the pivotal figure of the entire Royal Hospital enterprise. It was he who organized everything and was – in many ways – the true founder of the Hospital. He had served Charles in exile and had been found 'so honest and industrious, and withall so capable and ready' that in 1661 the King had appointed him Paymaster to the Forces.

The Paymaster was allowed £400 a year for himself and his clerks and deducted 2d. in the pound from soldiers' pay to cover Exchequer fees. But the system of payment for a Regular Army was in its infancy and, because revenues turned out to be inadequate, Army pay soon fell into arrears. Complaints were made against Fox – not for dishonesty but for a teething problem for which he was not responsible.

To solve the difficulty he agreed to issue pay to the soldiers weekly by borrowing the necessary funds. In return for pledging his own credit with his bankers, Fox charged the troops a commission of 1s. in the pound on their pay, as had been done in Ireland when Army pay had fallen behind there. One-third (4d.) was to cover Exchequer fees and his own expenses and two-thirds (8d.) was to cover the interest on the money that he would need to borrow. (The 'poundage' was taken from a soldier's 'off-takings', allocated to paying for uniform and other items, though in fact it was usually taken from his 'subsistence', which was supposed to be paid free of all deductions.) If Exchequer payments were outstanding after two months, Fox was to be allowed 8 per cent interest on the money he had advanced.

By careful management of his affairs Fox amassed a considerable fortune and naturally he had enemies. The Lord Treasurer, the Earl of Danby, sacked him as Paymaster in 1676 but three years later Danby was impeached and himself sacked while Fox was reinstated as 'the only instrument that has kept things afloat by his credit and supplies'.

Fox was indispensable but in 1679 he was appointed a Treasury Commissioner and resigned from the Pay Office, appointing as his nominees – to act on his behalf – his nephew Nicholas Johnson and his son William. Together these two men filled the office of Paymaster until, by April 1682, both were dead, when the post was filled by another of Fox's sons, Charles. Sir Stephen was thus able to exercise control over his old office through his successors.

In 1680 Evelyn believed Sir Stephen Fox to be worth at least £200,000, 'honestly gotten and unenvied, which is next to a miracle'. With that, 'he continues as humble and ready to do a courtesie as ever he was'. Virtuous and religious, he was behind the creation of several charitable foundations including an almshouse in his home town of Farley in Wiltshire, with the design of which Wren may have been involved.

On 22nd December 1681 Letters Patent were published announcing the King's intention of erecting a hospital for the relief of soldiers grown old or infirm in the service of the Crown, and 'to endow the same with a Revenue suitable thereunto'.

OPPOSITE: *Portico to Figure Court, an engraving by J. Collins of c. 1690 after an original drawing. Wren conceived the portico as a great gate – or triumphal arch – standing astride a long axial route from Kensington to Chelsea.*

The Paymaster-General, Fox's nephew Nicholas Johnson, was appointed Treasurer.

Three weeks later – on 11th January 1682 – Chelsea was secured. Wren reported to the Council of the Royal Society that, subject to its ratification, a deal had been agreed with Fox. Despite the fact that the offer was £200 below the asking price the Council approved. The £1,300 was paid by Fox out of his own pocket.

On 27th January 1682 Evelyn met Fox and wrote in his diary:

> This evening Sir Ste. Fox acquainted me againe with his Majestys resolution of proceeding in the erection of a Royal Hospital for emerited souldiers on that spot of ground which the Royal Society had sold to his Majesty for £1,300, and that he would settle £5,000 per ann. on it, and build to the value of £20,000 for the reliefe and reception of 4 companies, viz. 400 men, to be as in a colledge or monasterie.
>
> I was therefore desir'd by Sir Stephen (who had not onely the whole managing of this, but was, as I perceiv'd, himselfe to be a grand benefactor, as well it became him who had gotten so vast an estate by the souldiers) to assist him, and consult what method to cast it in, as to the government.

Then and there, in Fox's study, they set down their thoughts – 'to be consider'd and digested better' before they were revealed to the King and Archbishop Sancroft – for the staffing of the Royal Hospital: 'we arranged the governor, chaplaine, steward, housekeeper, chirurgeon, cook, butler, gardener, porter, and other officers, with their several salaries and entertainments'. Evelyn added, 'I would needes have a Library, and mention'd several books, since some souldiers might possibly be studious when they were at leisure to recollect'. The Hospital was to be run in every respect as strictly as any religious institution and Fox asked Evelyn to consider the laws and orders that would be required for governing it.

At this meeting much of the structure and organization of the future Hospital was discussed. But had an architect yet been appointed? Wren, as Surveyor-General of the King's Works, was the obvious choice and at some time between the sale of the Chelsea site in early January 1682 and the meeting between Evelyn and Fox later in the month he was appointed. It would seem that by 27th January Wren had even produced a draft, exploratory plan – no doubt responding to an initial brief from Fox, Evelyn, the King and his various advisers. Certainly a memorandum produced by Fox – which is undated

J. Collins Sculp.

but was almost certainly written at or immediately after the meeting with Evelyn – appears to be, in part, a response to a draft design already in existence.

In Fox's handwriting the memorandum is divided into four sections:

1. Objects and revenue.
2. The Pensioners, viz '4 Companys consisting off, In all, 384 Private Sentinells, 8 Drummers, 12 Corporalls, 8 Serjeants, 4 Ensigns, 4 Lts. 1 Martiall and Adjutant, 1 Governor, being 422 military persons'.
3. The twenty-nine proposed staff, 'For the Generall use & service of the forementioned society', including an apothecary, wardrobe keeper, porter, baker and brewer, and thirteen women to wash the linen and clean the house.
4. Estimate of salaries and expenses, totalling £7,748. 12s. 11d. per annum (£5,578 for the military and £1,075 for the 'usefull persons'). This sum included fuel, candles, medicines and tools for the gardener; 6d. a day was to be allowed for '32 Fires to the Chimneys of the private Centinells'.

Fox seems to have envisaged the Pensioners organized in traditional military units complete with the standard numbers of non-commissioned officers (NCOs), drummers and officers. So it was to be an establishment for all ranks – not just private soldiers – to operate as companies as in any line regiment. The very fact that the Pensioners are referred to as sentinels – or guards – hints at the function Fox intended them to fulfil, giving credence to the notion that the Hospital was conceived from the first as a barracks for a corps of royal bodyguards.

The number of chimneys referred to is the precise number eventually provided: a lucky guess, the number specified in a subsequent brief or – as is more likely – the number shown in a draft plan that Fox had in front of him when writing the memorandum.

In February 1682 the conveyance of old Chelsea College from the Royal Society to the Crown was completed and, in the same month, the King laid the foundation stone of the new building. Wren had evidently completed his designs to the extent that the location, form and size of the building were known. Certainly, from 1st March 1682, Leonard Gammon – Wren's Clerk of Works at Whitehall – was paid an additional £20 per annum as Clerk of Works at Chelsea, so it must be assumed that works had already

ABOVE: *The main, north front of the Royal Hospital. Stone was used for the quoins, and wood and plaster painted to look like stone for entablatures and cornices. Red-brick dressings contrast with the grey/purple brick to form the principal decorative feature of the building.*

started or were about to start. These would have involved a survey of the site, demolition of the existing building (with reusable materials salvaged) and preparation for the construction of new buildings. But it was not until 25th May 1682 that the final approval was gained.

On that day, wrote Evelyn, 'I was desir'd by Sir Ste. Fox and Sir Christopher Wren to accompany them to Lambeth, with the plot and designs of the College to be built at Chelsey, to have the Abp.'s [Archbishop's] approbation. It was a Quadrangle of 200 foote square, after the dimensions of the larger Quadrangle at Christ Church, Oxford, for accommodation of 440 persons, with governor and officers. This was agreed on'.

By July 1682 the old buildings had been pulled down and on 4th August Evelyn went 'with Sir Stephen Fox to survey the foundations of the Royal Hospital begun at Chelsea'. In the same month an additional 17 acres of land, adjoining the site, were purchased from Lord Cheyne. By 1st March 1683 – a year after the project had started in earnest and seven months after construction had begun – the west wing of the main block had been completed. This was good going indeed and a tribute to the well-oiled machine that was Wren's office and to the highly efficient apparatus of finance created and run by Fox.

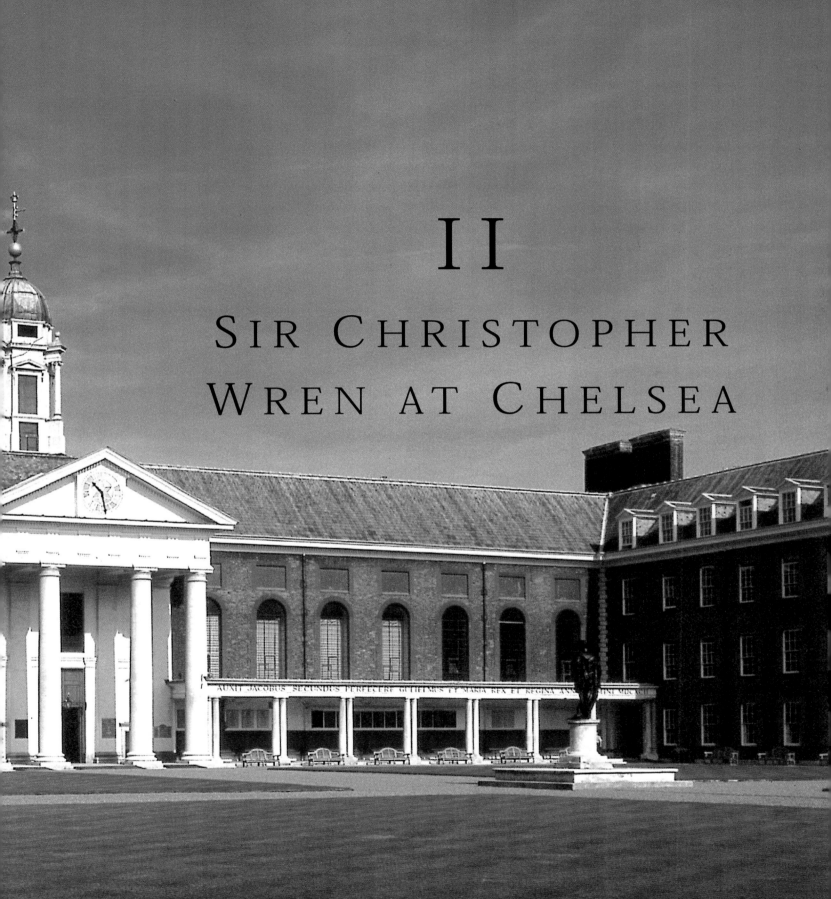

II

Sir Christopher
Wren at Chelsea

OPPOSITE: *View from beneath the portico showing a set of Wren's paired columns forming the colonnade attached to one of the giant columns of the portico. To the right is to be seen the residential wing on the west side of Figure Court containing the Pensioners' Long Wards.*

ABOVE: *Coat of arms of Sir Christopher Wren. Wren was knighted by Charles II in 1673 while work on St Paul's Cathedral was continuing and before he began to design the Royal Hospital.*

PREVIOUS PAGE: *South front of the Royal Hospital designed by Wren for Charles II, with the windows of the Great Hall to the left of the portico and of the Chapel to the right.*

WHEN WREN designed the Royal Hospital he had come a long way in his profession since – as a gifted amateur – he had designed his first buildings in Oxford and Cambridge. By 1682 his greatest work – St Paul's Cathedral – was almost a decade into construction, his brilliant Trinity College Library, Cambridge, was nearing completion and most of the fifty-two City churches to be rebuilt after the Great Fire of London in 1666 had been designed and many completed.

His office in New Scotland Yard was an immensely smooth-running, large and highly skilled organization. Many of the leading craftsmen of the late seventeenth century, such as Grinling Gibbons and Christopher Kempster, passed through, or worked directly for it. Nicholas Hawksmoor joined Wren's office in 1684 as his 'domestic clerk' and worked as a supervisor during the building of the Royal Hospital where, between 1687 and 1692, he was paid for 'drawing designs'.

No original drawings for the Royal Hospital survive however. Their loss is an unexplained mystery. As there is no mention of Chelsea in the list of drawings sold after Wren's death in 1723, they probably disappeared early on. But some time in early 1682 a memorandum was drafted – almost certainly by Wren himself – that outlined his vision for the Hospital:

> The two sides of ye Court are double building in three stories and garrets, both containing 16 galleries, in each of which are 24 cells divided off with partitions of wanscot, and two larger Cells for corporals . . . The upper end or front hath an Octagonall Vestibule in the middle covered with a Cupolo and Lanthorne 130 fot high, and before it a Portico of Dorick order . . . on each hand of which are lower Porticos leading to each Wing. On each side of the Vestibule are assents to the Hall on one hand and the Chappell on the other . . . On the corners of the Building are 4 Pavilions . . . The lesser Porticoes and principal doorways are Portland Stone. The rest of the Fabrick is brick, and the whole pile well and durably built with good materials.

Adjoining the main building were to be 'enclosures of brickwalls for Wallks, Gardens, Kitchin garden, Back Courte and Buriall place'. This describes the Royal Hospital essentially as it was built.

It was to be in the form of a 'colledge or monasterie' and, as Evelyn suggested, Wren

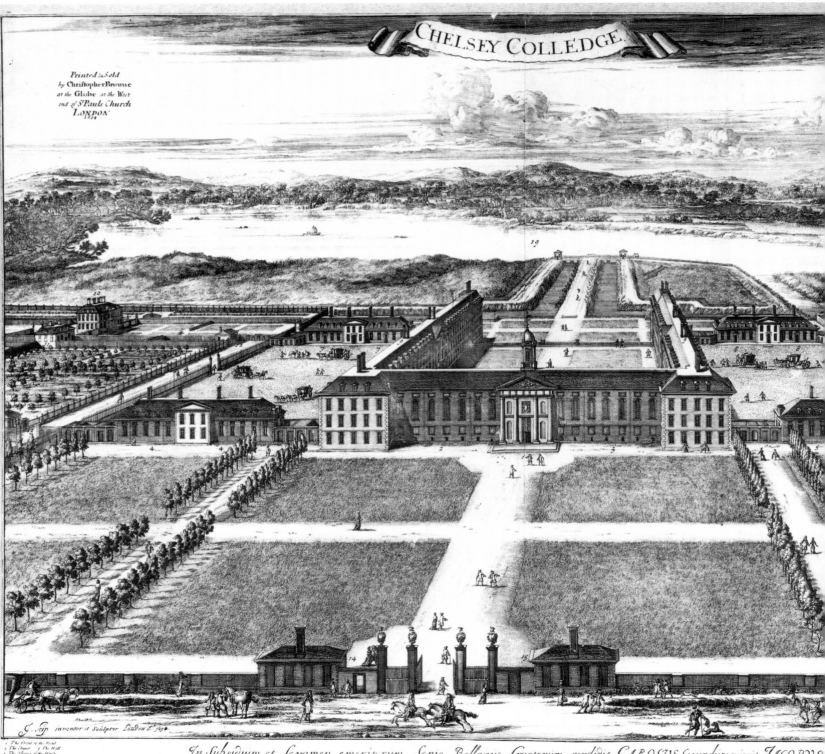

LEFT: *The Royal Hospital engraved by Johannes Kip in 1694. Lord Ranelagh stated in an account to the Commissioners in the spring of 1689, 'King William, upon his coming to the Crown, visited the said Hospital, and renewed the former directions for the speedy finishing and furnishing of it'.*

took his inspiration for the layout of the building from the colleges of Oxford. This is hardly surprising since he had been a student at Wadham College, taught in the University in the 1660s and between 1664 and 1669 constructed one of his earliest buildings there – the Sheldonian Theatre. The collegiate building form – with a central court or quadrangle, deriving from monastic design – incorporates a mixture of domestic and 'public' buildings and so was particularly appropriate for the Chelsea project. As in Oxford college buildings (notably New College and Wadham), Wren grouped the Great Hall and the Chapel together to form a dominant central feature of the composition.

But there was a major difference from the standard collegiate form. At Chelsea the court was defined by only three ranges: the fourth, south side, was left open. There were a few examples of this three-sided form in Oxford and Cambridge and Wren had a particular reason for adopting it here. It allowed the centre block, with its giant pedimented portico, to be seen from the Thames to the south and provided a good view of the river from the building.

A striking thing about Wren's building is its strange relationship to the river. Rather than confronting the Thames head-on, the Royal Hospital's central court (now known as Figure Court) sidles towards the river at an angle. Obviously Wren wanted the wards for the Pensioners in the two side ranges to be well lit and the orientation he chose means that none of the ranges looks directly north. And all the wards enjoy direct sunlight at some time during the day.

And then there is the evidence offered by the old Chelsea College building. This seems to have been oriented in the same manner and it is possible that Wren – always a pragmatist – simply wanted to utilize the foundations, roads and landscape of the old structure. But there is a more intriguing possibility – one that suggests Wren, in the early 1680s, nurtured a grandiose vision for the Baroque planning of west London.

The main axis around which the Royal Hospital is organized continues north-west to King's Road – a private royal road until 1830 that connected the court at Whitehall with Hampton Court Palace – which it contrives to hit neatly, if approximately, at right angles. This connection is now marked by Royal Avenue that continues the line of the north-west axis from the Hospital. It seems that in Wren's grand scheme King's Road was to be transformed into a major west–east axis through London – a great ornamental avenue linking the royal palaces at St James's and Whitehall with the Royal Hospital and, ultimately, Hampton Court Palace to the west. When William and Mary came to the throne in 1668 this plan was further developed.

The new monarchs, for reasons of health, politics and security, decided to use Whitehall Palace less and, instead, to occupy Hampton Court and a new palace in healthy and rural Kensington. For both the reconstruction and modernization of Hampton Court and for the new palace they chose Wren as architect. By 1690 Wren had approved the construction of a long straight road connecting Kensington Palace, on which work had started the previous year, with Whitehall.

The axis of the Royal Hospital, if continued north-west for nearly two miles, intersects the site of Wren's new Kensington Palace, so the placing of the palace provided Wren with the opportunity to create a long and majestic straight avenue between the two. A network of such avenues – intersecting, offering spectacular vistas and connecting royal palaces in Kensington and Whitehall with a loyal garrison at Chelsea – would have given a distinctly Baroque architectural character and royal flavour to west London. But this must remain speculation. All that is known for certain is that in 1693 Wren approved an estimate for a new road from Kensington Palace to the Royal Hospital at Chelsea. Royal Avenue – a strange, wide street now lined with early to mid-nineteenth-century houses – is the main physical evidence for this great Baroque town-planning scheme, hinting remotely at an urban grandeur that was never achieved, a victim to conflicts of interest and reluctance on the part of private landlords to co-operate.

In 1750 Wren's grandson published *Parentalia*, a history of the eminent members of the Wren family and Sir Christopher in particular. It includes Wren's somewhat random 'Tracts on Architecture', gathered together by his son. A section of the Tracts does, perhaps, explain one aspect of the Chelsea design: the visual accent on each range being placed in the centre – by means of columns and pediments – while the ends of each range have minimal emphasis. As Wren wrote, 'Fronts ought to be elevated in the Middle, not the Corners; because the Middle is the Place of greatest dignity, and first arrests the Eye; and rather projecting forward in the Middle, than hollow. For these Reasons, Pavilions at the Corners are naught; because they make both Faults, a hollow and depressed Front'.

Wren had no formal training as an architect nor did he come from a family of masons in which he would have been introduced to techniques of construction and design from an early age. He came from a family with traditions in the Church and universities and the young Wren – a don at Oxford with a genius for mathematics, science and astronomy – seems to have indulged his passion for architecture by studying influential books such as Sebastiano Serlio's *L'Architettura* and prints and travellers' sketches of Andrea Palladio's Venetian churches. His greatest direct architectural experience was a trip to Paris in 1665 (the only time he ever went abroad) which he undertook in order to extend his scientific experience and 'to survey the most esteem'd Fabricks of Paris'. He came back with his head full of all things French.

French classical architecture favoured great high-roofed pavilions – preferably at the centre but also at the corners of compositions. But in the Tract Wren dismissed pavilions

as 'naught'. He was moving away from France to something new, to something more his own creation. Chelsea is the first great expression in secular architecture of Wren's evolving national style.

The function of the two residential ranges of Figure Court is expressed – in a direct but subtle way – through the design and scale of their windows. In domestic architecture of the period the hierarchy of occupation could be read in the composition of the principal elevation. The grand rooms in the house – dining room or best parlour – would have higher ceilings than less grand rooms and so have larger windows. In important buildings of the period the main rooms were almost always grouped on the

ABOVE: *The north front and Doric frontispiece, with a view through the building to Figure Court and the statue of Charles II. Beneath the cupola and lantern is the Octagon Porch.*

first floor – the *piano nobile* of the Renaissance *palazzo* – so the windows on this level would be deeper, although the same width, as windows on other floors.

At the Royal Hospital Wren did not follow this convention – and for very good reason. The three main levels of the residential ranges are all of equal importance – they all contain wards for the Pensioners – so he designed the windows to be of equal depth. The practical and happy consequence of this rational decision was that he designed the windows on each floor to be as deep as possible, allowing the maximum amount of light to stream into the wards.

Above the cornice of the residential ranges rises a tall pitched roof furnished with slightly smaller dormer windows. This roof space contains a top, fourth tier of wards, creating the habitable space that was required to house the intended number of Pensioners.

The range containing the Great Hall and the Chapel is in every sense the centrepiece of the composition, as all its details proclaim. It is essentially a single-storey building – revealed by its massive semi-circular arched windows – so there is no doubt that it contains the major, public rooms of the Hospital. These huge, close-spaced windows give the building a dramatic transparency and allow light to flood inside.

The Doric frontispiece and portico – and their related internal and external details – form the great decorative, architectural and symbolic feature of the Royal Hospital. Built of stone and timber, painted to look like stone, these monumental portals stand in stark contrast to the generally domestic character of the brick building they adorn.

The large scale of the portals was utilized in a most practical manner by the pragmatic Wren, for he fitted cisterns within the pediments to supply water at some pressure to the lower rooms of the Hospital. In 1805 it was described how the water 'is worked up from the river, by a patent engine placed in a small building erected for that purpose in the gardens, near the river side'. The 'patent' engine was, presumably, a steam-powered pump.

The visual importance of these great Doric porches is confirmed by the interior into which they lead. Here Wren created a stunning composition of almost Neo-classical clarity. Octagonal in plan and rising to a faceted dome that is top-lit – like the Pantheon in Rome – by a central oculus, the Octagon Porch is effectively a temple to the military virtues – austere, simple, masculine. The walls are dressed with giant Doric pilasters that relate to the exterior columns and pilasters of the Doric porches. This continuation

of an exterior order internally was something that appealed to Wren – as it did to his fellow Baroque architects such as Sir John Vanbrugh and Nicholas Hawksmoor – when designing monumental interiors.

As well as being a military temple, this domed space also fulfils the more mundane function of entrance vestibule to both the Chapel and the Great Hall. These are a pair of spectacular rooms that, by their use, place the Royal Hospital firmly in the tradition of the academic college. As with Wren's Trinity College Library, the huge windows of the Great Hall and the Chapel have high sills to allow for the disposition of panelling or chapel seating against the lower levels of the wall.

The Chapel has a barrel vault with plaster embellishments by the Master Plasterer Henry Margetts. These are discreet but of high quality with the oblong plaster panels, set along the wall below the springing of the vault, being especially good. Each panel is of broadly similar design but in its details individual and inventive, many with strange faces lurking in the foliage.

LEFT: *Detail of the plasterwork in the Chapel. It was carried out in 1687 by the Master Plasterer Henry Margetts. 'For 16 Capitells with Lace leaves & Cherubinsheads' he charged £12 16s.*

RIGHT: *Limewood foliage panel from one of the gates in the altar rail carved by William Morgan.*

FAR RIGHT: *Corinthian capitals and part of the pediment of the altarpiece. The work was shared between the Master Carver William Emmett and William Morgan.*

The Hall was organized in the manner of a college hall or a medieval great hall. The Pensioners dined at sixteen long tables – one for each ward – and until 1740 the Governor and his guests dined at the high table raised on a shallow dais at the west end. In the medieval tradition, the highest in the Hospital dined with the lower orders.

One of the oddities of the Great Hall at Chelsea was that there was no door to connect it directly with the kitchen immediately to its west. Food had to be carried from the kitchen and along the colonnade to the south of the Hall and then through the octagonal entrance vestibule and so into the Hall from the east end. This was a most inconvenient arrangement but it did – and this was presumably the point – duplicate the traditional practice of parading food along the length of the Great Hall to the high table on the dais. This pomp was usually achieved by the simple device of placing the kitchen, scullery and buttery at the opposite end of the Hall to the dais. But Wren could not do this at the Royal Hospital for the Chapel occupied the traditional location of the kitchen offices. Clearly, when it came to dining, maintaining tradition and ritual was more important than mere function. By around 1805, however, a serving hatch had been created between the kitchen and Hall and by 1824 a full door – but by then the Great Hall had changed dramatically in its use.

ABOVE: *The Great Hall, which has portraits of British monarchs hung high on the walls. Above are replicas of captured flags and below are panels of battle honours. After damage in the Second World War the windows were glazed with rectangular-shaped panes to replace the diamond-shaped 'quarrels'.*

BELOW: *Detail of the plasterwork ceiling of the Parlour, now the Council Chamber, which was decorated by John Grove in 1687 with military emblems.*

ABOVE: *Detail of the finely carved picture frame surrounding the portrait of Charles I and his family that formed part of the original furnishings of the Governor's Parlour.*

OPPOSITE: *Mural painting in the Great Hall carried out by Antonio Verrio and Henry Cooke between 1688 and 1692. Charles II on horseback is crowned by the winged figure of Victory. In a cartouche is his cypher of intertwined 'C's, and in the background the Hospital buildings.*

Both the Chapel and the Hall were to contain mural paintings. That in the apse of the Chapel depicting the Resurrection is by Sebastiano Ricci working in collaboration with his nephew Marco Ricci. It was probably paid for by Queen Anne. The painting in the Hall is a more theatrical affair showing the triumph of the founder of the Royal Hospital – Charles II – on horseback surrounded by allegorical figures. It was begun by Antonio Verrio and completed by Henry Cooke.

The spaces above and below the vast volumes of the Chapel and the Hall were put to good, practical use. The roof space above the Hall was used, initially, as accommodation for the nurses – the 'matrons', as they were then called – and that above the Chapel as a store room. The brick vaulted undercrofts below both were used by the Usher of the Hall as a brewery and store for 300 barrels holding a six-week supply of beer.

While the plan of the Royal Hospital was derived from that of an Oxford college, the elevations were conceived within the convention of palace façades – that is to say

ABOVE: *Details of military trophies from the limewood overmantel in the Council Chamber carved by William Emmett. The original account – he was paid £30 in 1687 – describes the piece as 'painfully wrought'.*

ABOVE: *The Council Chamber.*
The portrait of Sir Stephen Fox
over the mantelpiece, which was
installed in 1776 by Robert
Adam when he was Clerk of
Works, is flanked by portraits by
Sir Peter Lely of Charles II,
Catherine of Braganza and
James II as Duke of York.

each range was given a pedimented feature in its centre and subservient pavilions at its
ends. These pavilions are cubes, four windows wide, fulfilling very different roles. That
to the north-east absorbs the apse of the Chapel and contains a most oddly shaped
vestry room. That to the north-west contained the kitchen for the Great Hall. Those to
the south were designed to contain apartments for officers of the Royal Hospital – with
that to the south-east being the grandest of all since it provided residential and reception
rooms for the Governor.

At ground-floor level was the Governor's Parlour (now the Council Chamber), one
of the best of Wren's surviving domestic interiors. It is a reminder that Wren – through
his City commissions and as Surveyor-General of the King's Works – had trained, and
had access to, the leading craftsmen of the land. The Parlour is panelled in oak (provided
by William Cleere, Master Joiner to the Office of Works), has an overmantel embellished
with delicate carving (by William Emmett and William Morgan) and a fine plaster ceiling

(by John Grove, Master Plasterer to the Office of Works). The motifs in both the plaster- and timberwork date the creation of the room; indeed the ceiling contains elaborate mouldings displaying the cypher of James II, as does the carved overmantel, revealing that the room was completed between 1685 and 1688. Perhaps the most remarkable thing about the room is its volume. It measures 40 feet (12m.) long by 30 feet (9m.) wide and is almost as high as it is wide, thus creating a room that corresponds to Palladio's ideal proportion of a cube and a third.

At the beginning of February 1685, days before Charles II died and when the building had just been fully roofed,

> His Majestie . . . was glad to see it & said to the Company then with Him on the place, That Fox and Hee had done that great worke without the help of the Treas[ur]y, who indeed never gave the least countenance towards it; For it was carried on by His Majesty's giving out of his Privy purse (at that time but £16,000 p. Ann.) in remote Tallys on the Hearth money £7,000 with interest due thereon, and Sr Ste Fox's Fund of 4d. in the pound.

Since the Treasury stood aloof from funding this building, money had to come from elsewhere. Primarily – as this later account by Fox suggests – from the King himself, who used revenues from a tax then levied on householders in England that was assessed on the number of hearths – or fireplaces – in each house. This was a crude form of income or wealth tax based on the notion that the size of a house could be calculated from the number of hearths it contained and that the larger the house the richer the owner or occupier. The money was contributed from what was known as the King's 'Secret Service' fund.

'Fox's Fund' is a reference to Sir Stephen Fox's scheme for using the poundage deductions on soldiers' pay for the Hospital. The loan arrangement for paying the Army came to an end in December 1680 and from that date two-thirds of the money was at the disposal of the King. In 1683 Fox arranged for one half of this sum (4d.), backdated to 1861, to be devoted to the Hospital and later the other half. Thus 8d. in the pound deducted from soldiers' pay (about £8,000 a year) would go towards the Hospital. As well as paying for the site, Fox himself lent up to £10,000 without interest so that Wren could negotiate contracts with masons and other craftsmen.

RIGHT: *Four 'rich Girandoles', decorated with festoons and military trophies and gilded, were acquired for Robert Adam's redecoration of the Governor's Parlour. Reflected in the glass of one of the two surviving girandoles is the portrait of Catherine of Braganza, wife of Charles II.*

The King's delight in the Hospital when he saw it in February 1685 seems to have been partly due to the way he and Fox had triumphed over the severe problem of providing money for the Hospital. Concern for economy was always an issue at Chelsea.

Essentially, Wren's buildings divide into two types: those that were grand because funds were plentiful and those that were modest because the use, brief or site demanded it or because of lack of money. Wren's modest style can be seen best in a number of his plainer City churches (for example St Benet's, Paul's Wharf; St Anne and St Agnes; and the design of St James's, Piccadilly) and – of course – at the Royal Hospital. This approach was to be developed by Wren – in a fascinating manner – in the late 1680s and 1690s when he was commissioned by William and Mary to design Kensington Palace.

Wren achieved this visual modesty and economy through simplicity of design and through his choice of materials. These buildings are characterized by the use of brick construction (always executed with exquisite craftsmanship), with more expensive stone used only for quoins, doorcases and, occasionally, for columns and pilasters. These are the 'good materials' that are mentioned in the 1682 memorandum describing the Hospital. Other elements, such as entablatures and cornices, are of timber and plaster painted to look like stone.

At the Royal Hospital the main ornament comprises the handsome and well-laid grey/purple bricks, the most striking decorative detail being the red-brick dressings and delicate cut-brick arches that frame each window opening. This is a simple and bold structural ornament that was to be adopted by London builders and remain popular into the 1730s.

Within three years of work starting on the construction of the Royal Hospital the man behind its foundation and financing was dead. Charles II died on 6th February 1685 and with his death – and the ascent to the throne of his brother James II – turbulent times rapidly returned to Britain. Foolishly James attempted to re-establish Roman Catholicism and a type of absolute monarchy. He did not realize the extent to which the times – and the temper of the nation – had changed. Nor did he seem to understand the essential weakness of his own position. By 1688 the experiment was over and James had been forced to flee – in most ignominious circumstances – to be replaced by the Dutch Protestant Prince of Orange and his wife, Mary Stuart.

These three short years were eventful. The Duke of Monmouth, mentioned earlier, led a bloody and unsuccessful Protestant rebellion in the West Country. Monmouth's uncle, James II, made the young man pay with his life for this adventure. This revolt no doubt confirmed James in his determination to enlarge the size of the Standing Army.

This decision had a direct and dramatic influence on the Royal Hospital. First, it meant that the Hospital's revenue automatically increased since, with an increase in military manpower, there was an increase in the number of soldiers' salaries that, in line with poundage reductions, provided the Hospital with its income. Second, with an enlarged army, there was urgent need for additional accommodation at Chelsea because there would be more invalids qualifying for entry than had been anticipated.

The position in 1685 is explained in a contemporary document:

> When King James came to the Crowne, the Forces were rais'd to above double the number of what they were in His Brother's time. So that there was a deduction of about £12,000 p. ann. out of the Pay of the Army for the said Hospitall, upon which Fund Sr Ste: Fox and Sr Chris: Wren did settle the Establishment for the maintenance of about 500 soldiers, besides the Officers & everything relating to the Hospitall.

So, even before the building was completed, it had to be enlarged to accommodate 500 men rather than the original 422. To raise additional funds for the work – and for veterans awaiting admission – the King levied a tax that had been proposed by Fox during the previous reign but not put into effect: the stoppage of a day's pay per annum from every officer and soldier in the Army. This deduction continued until 1783.

In November 1685 Sir Thomas Ogle was appointed Governor of the Royal Hospital. This was, essentially, a military position. Garrison towns and fortresses had governors and the Crown-appointed Governor of the Royal Hospital was to act like the colonel of a regiment and, with his veteran troops, was clearly expected to fulfil an active role if necessary.

With the need to expand the courtyard design of the Hospital Wren quickly saw that the solution lay in his initial concept of a family of buildings, with the three ranges of the central courtyard surrounded by minor buildings fulfilling subordinate functions. The extra accommodation could be provided in smaller ranges added – in appropriate manner – to the main ranges.

Governor

'THE ROYAL HOSPITAL IS RATHER LIKE A zoo,' explains the Governor, Sir Jeremy Mackenzie GCB OBE, 'people love to look at it, but we have to make sure the gorgeous animals inside are happy.' This playful comment reflects a great truth about the potentially conflicting demands that characterize life in the Royal Hospital. It has become one of the great – and best loved – institutions in Britain, housing about 350 veteran soldiers in some of the most handsome and important historic buildings in the land.

'We are proud of our buildings,' says the Governor, 'but the jewel in our crown is the Pensioners. Without them this would be just another big, empty, beautiful historic building looking for a new use.' And to ensure that the Royal Hospital continues to attract the veterans some tough decisions have to be made, and some serious money raised. This is the type of challenge that appeals to Sir Jeremy.

Originally the Governor held the job for life and this could – and did – lead to some odd states of affairs. 'There was one Governor,' remembers Sir Jeremy, 'who had to go around with a label attached to his sleeve: "If found, please return to the Royal Hospital", and whose batman danced an Irish jig to entertain visitors.' Now Governors are limited to six years' service and, during the last few decades, have evolved an increasingly professional approach to the job.

'The Commissioners own the place and I'm the Commissioner responsible to the other Commissioners for its day-to-day running. I'm responsible for the continuity of the Royal Hospital, for making sure that we find people to live here.' The expression of this obligation is the opening-up of the Royal Hospital to the public, and the determination to see its buildings and history as a resource that can be used to help fund the changes that Sir Jeremy sees as not only inevitable but essential. Increasingly the Royal Hospital has engaged with life outside its walls; it is becoming more open and it is advancing the policy of making itself as financially independent as possible.

The changes that Sir Jeremy is initiating – and for which funds must be raised through an appeal – are daunting. The Long Wards have to be modernized if the Royal Hospital is to continue to attract residents. These works will, inevitably, involve many problems in reconciling the demands of the historic fabric with those of modern comfort and convenience. But more difficult still is the first priority – the creation of a new and larger Infirmary to replace the 1960s building. This must fit in with the buildings of Wren and Soane while containing the most modern medical facilities – and the result must please not only the In-Pensioners and staff of the Royal Hospital but the architectural establishment, the people of Chelsea and all who pass by.

The Governor has to be an inspired leader, a gracious host, a skilful fund-raiser and an astute politician as well as fulfilling his traditional role as the head of a quasi-military establishment.

The progress of the Hôtel des Invalides was closely studied with, no doubt, Wren getting hold of Le Jeune de Boullencourt's well-illustrated *Description Générale de l'Hostel Royal des Invalides* of 1683. Not only did the Invalides have a military Governor – probably providing the model for Chelsea – but it included accommodation for cavalry officers of the Garde du Corps. So, in this new building at Chelsea Wren provided rooms for gentlemen of the Life Guards. Now the men and NCOs of the Royal Hospital were to be stiffened by a number of resident cavalry officers.

Wren did what now seems obvious. He created four buildings of identical appearance that – although only one storey above ground – are noble in design. With their taller centre pediments, high-pitched and dormered roofs and tall chimney stacks, they are smaller versions of the main ranges. Wren placed these four new ranges or wings with a pair facing each other to the west of the main ranges and the second pair facing each other on the east.

The pairs of wings were to form two additional courts equal in area to that of the main court, with their western and eastern edges defined by simple, single-storey and freestanding end pavilions housing minor uses and walls screening mundane activities. One of the four new ranges was to serve as an Infirmary, an innovation that seems to reflect a rapidly increasing concern for the welfare of the inmates. It contained thirty-three beds and three 'cradle' beds.

The conception of the enlarged Hospital as both a functioning and a veteran military unit is confirmed by a description of 1688, the year that James II fled. It is clear that the Royal Hospital was, at one level, to be regarded as the barracks of a regiment of foot:

> That the 416 foot to be lodged in the 16 gallearies already finished may be put into eight companies for their better government & doing of duty, each company to be made up of the men of two gallaries, being 52 in number (viz.) 4 serjeants & 48 private soldiers.
>
> That the Horse granadiers & light horse may be also put into a company to be called a company of patizans or a company of fuziliers. That each of the said 9 companies may have a captain, lieutenant & ensign, to be taken out of the 30 officers, and that the remaining 3 officers be colonel, lieut-colonel and major to the said 9 companies.

The setting that Wren created for the Royal Hospital was of the greatest importance and it was during the reign of James II that work on the grounds began. The buildings were to sit within a bold and simple landscape that – in its orthogonal geometry – complemented the regularity of the buildings and reinforced the impression that the Royal Hospital was a key component in a great axial plan for west London.

The organization of the landscape is very well shown in a plan and a perspective of 1694 (see pages 26 and 36). Not only was the main axis of the Hospital continued north-west to King's Road across Burton's Court (laid out with oblong parterres divided by a grid of gravel walks), but it was also extended south-east and used to organize the gardens lying between the Royal Hospital and the Thames.

The gardens were a restrained exercise in the French formal style by George London and Henry Wise, who were also responsible for their cultivation and maintenance. The courtyard enclosed by the Hospital was echoed to its south by a square of identical area and design, but unrestrained by buildings except at its north corners where it was defined by the end pavilions of the Wren range. This subtle bit of wit – making a play of negative and positive spaces (the buildings are the most important element in one square and the space in the other) – was continued south by a broad walk that continued the main

LEFT: *Eighteenth-century engraving of the kitchen garden to the south of Wren's Infirmary with a dovecote in the foreground.*

axis of the Hospital. This central walk was flanked by narrower straight walks shaded by avenues of trees. To the west and east of these walks were utilitarian gardens for growing vegetables and herbs and containing rows of fruit trees.

The most spectacular feature of these southern gardens was a pair of right-angled canals that, in effect, brought the Thames right up to the southern terrace of the Hospital. The river edge of the garden was terraced and walled to form a raised walk and furnished with a water gate and a pair of cubical end pavilions. It was all very handsome and useful.

Road works in the nineteenth century did great damage. The Thames Embankment – constructed between 1850 and 1868 – wrecked the southern gardens by demolishing the riverside terrace and its related structures and by cutting the Hospital off from the Thames, while, to the north, the construction of Royal Hospital Road severed the building from Burton's Court. These sad alterations have greatly reduced the visual excitement of the Royal Hospital for it no longer stands – as intended – at the centre of a wide and coherent Baroque landscape.

Although work on the building itself was finished by 1689, the veterans were prevented from moving into the Royal Hospital by the deviousness and scheming of Richard Jones, Earl of Ranelagh. Lord Ranelagh had challenged Fox's claim to perquisites from military pay and, in December 1685, followed Sir Stephen's son Charles as Paymaster-General and Treasurer of the Royal Hospital. If Sir Stephen Fox and his two sons had been discreet and restrained in the use of their position, Ranelagh was not.

One of Ranelagh's first actions was to create an official residence for himself in the grounds and in about 1688 a fine, freestanding mansion – following Wren's design for the main buildings – had been begun, to the east of the main court.

In April 1691, when William III dined at the Royal Hospital, the Paymaster managed to gain only one favour for the Royal Hospital – the grant to himself as its Treasurer of a salary of £1 a day, backdated to 1685. Not only was the long overdue opening of the Hospital not discussed at this meeting but, it seems, Ranelagh was doing his best to delay the opening. He realized that he would be unable to continue to embellish his own house and gardens, using money for the main building, once the Hospital had been taken into use and its future revenue settled.

This unpleasant situation was finally sorted out – probably by Sir Stephen Fox and Sir Christopher Wren working closely with Queen Mary and the Secretary of State, the Earl of Nottingham. First, Royal Warrants were issued in 1691 that renewed the allocation to the Royal Hospital of two-thirds of the Army poundage fund – and so the issue was taken out of Ranelagh's hands. This was dated retrospectively from the beginning of 1688 so that over £60,000 became available immediately to complete and open the Hospital. Then, to ensure that Ranelagh had only a very limited opportunity to misbehave in future, another Royal Warrant was issued – in August 1691 – that transferred the management of the Royal Hospital from Ranelagh to an executive committee composed of Lord Ranelagh, Sir Stephen Fox and Sir Christopher Wren.

Ranelagh proved himself to be the archetypal plausible rogue. He was constantly instructed to submit accounts and just as constantly failed to do so. Further warrants were issued to reduce his authority but Ranelagh managed to ingratiate himself with William III, who appointed him a Privy Councillor and so bolstered his position. It was evident to all that Ranelagh was embezzling – or at the very least mismanaging – Hospital funds, particularly by retaining money that should have been spent on out-pensions. He continued to dodge and duck until 1702 when, on the accession of Queen Anne, the Committee of Public Accounts was instructed to investigate Ranelagh's conduct and debt to the Army.

Despite the absence of Ranelagh's Hospital accounts the committee eventually reported that he was guilty of gross fraud. But in December 1702 – before the committee

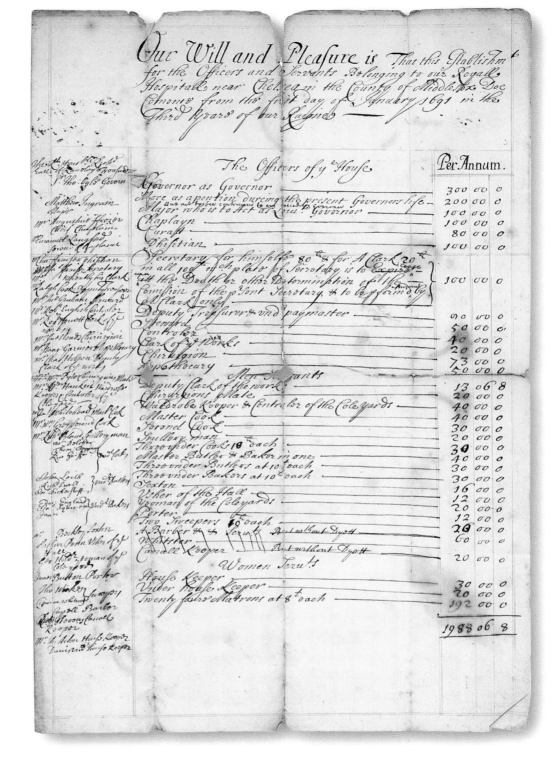

RIGHT: *Royal Warrant of William III in the Museum at the Royal Hospital listing the officers and servants and their annual rates of pay.*

had come to this conclusion but realizing what was in store – Ranelagh resigned as Paymaster-General and, two months later, was expelled from the House of Commons. Thereafter he moved gradually into a world of increasing debt although, despite his record, he managed to secure official appointments of an inferior sort.

Throughout all this Ranelagh managed to hang on to his house. Although built with embezzled Hospital funds he had secured a sixty-one-year lease in April 1690 at a rent of £15. 7s. 8d. – and this included not just the 'Mansion House' but 'all other Houses, Buildings Barnes, Stables and Dovehouses' that stood on the seven and a half acres of land that he had allocated himself. In 1697 he succeeded in obtaining a grant in perpetuity of all the land then in his possession, including an additional fifteen acres leased to him in 1693 that covered land now occupied by Chelsea Barracks. The grant was made as a settlement on Ranelagh's second wife and to compensate him for losses caused by the war in Ireland and was subject to a rent of £5 per annum.

As for Wren, for his ten years of magnificent work – and upon the submission of his correctly audited bills – he was awarded a modest £1,000 in June 1693.

RIGHT: *Detail of one of Wren's wings showing the cornice and the dormer windows of the top, fourth storey.*

III

The Chelsea Pensioners

OPPOSITE: *View down a Long Ward, only slightly altered from Wren's original design. Two wards are arranged back to back on each floor of the four floors of the east and west wings. The Pensioners' oak-panelled cabins are linked to form a continuous elevation with the entrance to each defined by Doric pilasters.*

ABOVE: *Detail from a painting of the Battle of the Boyne painted by Jan Wyck in 1690 celebrating the victory of his Protestant fellow-countryman William III over James II and his Catholic forces. The battle ended James's campaign to regain the English throne.*

PREVIOUS PAGE: *Hand-coloured aquatint of Chelsea Pensioners eating in the Great Hall, from* The Microcosm of London, *published from 1808 to 1810. For this series of plates the architecture was drawn by Augustus Charles Pugin and the figures by Thomas Rowlandson.*

THE VETERANS eventually started to arrive in February 1692. Earlier in the year soldiers eligible through twenty or more years of service or through infirmity had been inspected by the 'Generall officers' of the Army in order to identify those fit for garrison duty. On 4th February a list was made of 'Souldiers Disabled by their Wounds now in the Royal Hospital of King Charles ye 2cond'. Most of the men were severely wounded, lacked limbs or were lame and of the ninety-nine named twenty-five were in the Infirmary.

In return for accommodation the In-Pensioners (the Chelsea Pensioners living 'in' the Hospital) surrendered their Army pensions, retaining only a fragment as pocket money. Their pensions, with the poundage on soldiers' pay, were originally one of the principal sources of revenue for the Royal Hospital and it remains a condition of entry to this day that In-Pensioners surrender their Army pensions.

The only major battle fought by English soldiers during the period when the Hospital was under construction was – with bitter irony – between two of the Royal Hospital patrons. James II and his 'Jacobite' army met, and were soundly beaten by, William III at the Battle of the Boyne in July 1690. Some of William's 2,000 casualties, with veterans of the Civil War, must have formed part of the first Chelsea intake.

In a manner that was entirely in character, Wren gave careful consideration to the Pensioners' living quarters, known as the Long Wards. Each floor in the residential ranges consists of two wards placed back to back with the cabins set against the inner spine wall. The panelled cabins were originally only 6 feet (1.8m) square but they offered a degree of privacy unprecedented at the time. The remaining space, lit by deep windows and heated by two great fireplaces in each ward, would serve, essentially, as an internal 'street' and as a mess area.

Each ward was designed to house twenty-four Pensioners under the command of two NCOs – or 'Ward Captains' as they soon came to be called – making twenty-six berths in total. Two wards were the equivalent of one company, so the military formation of the In-Pensioners was reflected in their sleeping arrangements. In an emergency this would make it easy for the NCOs to rouse, rally and brief their men. The wide open-well staircases with shallow treads were designed to allow the crippled or infirm to ascend and descend to their wards with the greatest possible ease.

Wren placed groups of privies – over cesspits – at the ends of the later single-storey wings. It would seem that, from the start, there was concern about the ability of all the veterans to negotiate the route and consequently each ward was provided with eight brass pails and one pewter chamber pot. In 1739 the Board considered the provision of

OPPOSITE: *Each residential wing is served by a staircase at each end of the wards. Constructed of oak, they have stout balusters and shallow risers to make a gradual ascent for the Pensioners.*

ABOVE: *A number and name plate above the doorway of a berth in one of the Long Wards.*

closets within the main building to avoid the evils of going to the 'Bog' houses and finally, in 1790, two close stools were fitted in each of the 'washing places' in the porticoes. In 1829 two water closets were fitted on each floor of the main residential ranges.

During the 1680s – while the Royal Hospital was under construction but before it was occupied – arrangements started to be made for the organization and clothing of the veterans. Most of these were entirely in accord with current military and regimental practice and confirming that the men were still viewed as serving soldiers. Responsibility for the existing corps of Army Pensioners – who mostly lodged on an ad hoc basis in and around Westminster – was given to Captain Matthew Ingram, a half-pay officer. The men were paid daily, with the only deduction being for their clothing. At this time they wore the uniforms of their regiments, and many would have been little more than rags. But by Christmas 1685 Ingram had got matters in hand.

Using the clothing deductions, uniforms were manufactured and these were of distinctive design. Ingram had obtained permission to put the veterans into Royal Livery, so, like the men of royal regiments, they wore the standard 1685 pattern long red coats with dark blue facings. The sixty or so staff appointed to attend them had also to be clothed in a decent and uniform manner. The first uniform designed specifically for the Royal Hospital was that of the Porter – an important post since he was the most visible 'public face' of the Hospital. This 'Livery Cloath', created in about 1687, was 'a lavish affair of green with a mass of gold lace frogging.

By the time the first Chelsea Pensioners were in occupation the uniform arrangements had been slightly refined. They were now clothed in one of two types of uniform – standard infantry or standard cavalry depending on the arm in which they had served. The only non-standard detail was that – until William III's death in 1702 – a royal cypher ('W' entwined with 'M') was placed on the backs of the coats of all ranks, while in the Regular Army only drummers' and bandsmen's coats were adorned with the cypher.

A description of these uniforms from 1692 survives. The lower grade infantry uniform was 'a red Cloth Coat wth. Brass Buttons lined with blew Bays & False sleeves, wth. a large Cypher of the King and Queen on the Back, And blew Kersey Breeches . . . [a] Black hat with Copper [gold tinsel] Edgings & white hair hatbands'. The portrait of William Hiseland (see page 95), shows this uniform in good detail.

Long Ward Maid

MARIA VERELA HAS BEEN A Long Ward Maid for twenty-eight years. She looks after thirty-six men in two of the upper wards, where the fittest Pensioners tend to be housed. 'One wants the window open, another wants it closed, they argue, I laugh, we sort the problem out.' Sometimes the men become melancholy and Maria raises their spirits; sometimes they can't sleep and wander round the ward all night, disturbing and dismaying their fellow Pensioners, and Maria has to quieten things down. She has developed a profound respect and affection for the old soldiers she has cared for. 'For me this is the best job in the world. Life here is like in a village. We have everything we need.'

Men Servants

Lamp Lighter	20
Surgeon's Mate	20
Surgeon's Deputy	20
Comptroler of the Coal Yard	20
More to him for a Servant to deliver the Coals instead of the Yeoman.	10
With Diet Wardrobe Keeper	20
Master Baker and 3 Servants	50
Master Cook	40
Second Cook	30
Three Under Cooks, at £10. each	30
Master Butler and Servants	40
Under Butler	25
Barber and Servants	60
Scullery Man	20
Two Under Scullery Men at £10. each	20
Sexton	20
Usher of the Hall	20
Porter	12
Canal Keeper and Turn Cock	20
Gardiner	20
Messenger	20
with Diet Two Sweepers at £10. each	20
Organist	20
For repairing and Tuning the Organ	6
For Keeping the Clock	6
For Keeping the Water Engine in repair	20
To the Rector of Chelsea for Tyths & Rent	18 : 9
To the Vicar of Kensington for Tyths	2

Women Servants

With Diet House Keeper	30
24 Matrons at £8. each	192
Carried forward	2607 : 9

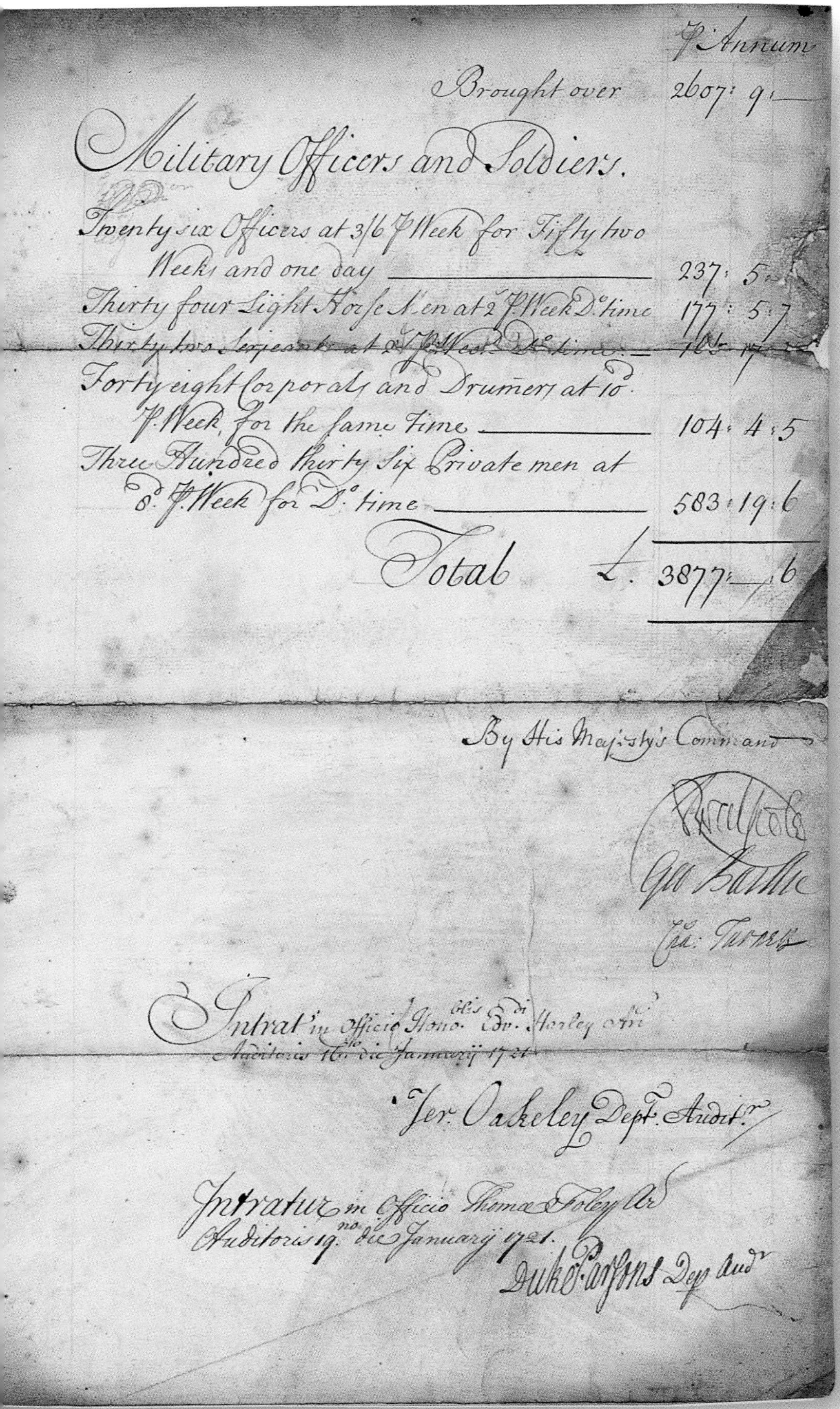

℘ Annum

Brought over 2607: 9: —

Military Officers and Soldiers.

Twenty six Officers at 3/6 ℘ Week for Fifty two Weeks and one day	237: 5:
Thirty four Light Horse Men at 2s ℘ Week Do time	177: 5: 7
~~Thirty two Serjeants at 2s ℘ Week Do time~~	~~166: 17~~
Forty eight Corporals and Drumers at 10d ℘ Week, for the same Time	104: 4: 5
Three Hundred thirty Six Private men at 8d ℘ Week for Do time	583: 19: 6
Total £	3877: —: 6

By His Majesty's Command

Geo Baillie

Tho: Turner

Intrat' in Officio Honobis Edri Harley Armi Auditoris 16to die January 1721

Jer. Oakeley Dept. Auditr

Intratur in Officio Thomæ Foley Ar Auditoris 19no die January 1721.

Duke Parsons Dep Audr

LEFT: *Page from the Royal Hospital accounts for the year 1756 listing payments to servants, including the Comptroller of the Coal Yard and Canal Keeper, officers and 336 soldiers; also the cost of repairing and tuning the organ and keeping the water engine in repair.*

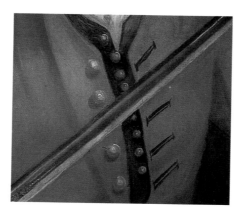

LEFT: *Detail from the portrait of William Hiseland. It shows the red cloth coat edged in blue and brass buttons of the infantry In-Pensioners' uniform as originally designed in 1692.*

The cavalry coat – typical of that worn by horse regiments – was 'a Crimson Cloth Coat with large Brass Buttons, lined with blew Serge, the Sleeves turned up with ye same Cloth & bound about with gold Braid; and a pair of Breeches of blew . . . A Black Hat with gold Edgings and a white hair hatband'.

Initially Pensioners who had served as sergeants in infantry regiments wore cavalry uniforms identical to those worn by Light Horsemen. This must have been very confusing and in about 1703 infantry sergeants were distinguished from cavalrymen by pewter buttons and by silver braid on their sleeves, pockets and hats. It seems that at this time blue waistcoats were also issued.

In 1692 the In-Pensioner officers wore 'a Scarlet Cloth Coat with Gilt Brass Buttons, lined with blew Shalloon. The Sleeves turn'd up with the same Cloth & bound about with gold Braid, & a pair of Breeches of fine blew Cloth . . . a Black hat edged with the same Lace as ye Sleeves, & a gold Hatband'.

From 1707 each Pensioner was issued – once every three years – with a greatcoat or 'surtout' of dark blue with scarlet or crimson facings for upper ranks. This additional and most useful garment was provided through a trust established by Lord Ranelagh. The trust operated into the 1940s so that generations of In-Pensioners owed their winter warmth to the otherwise disreputable Ranelagh.

James II had authorized the formation of Invalid Companies from among the Pensioners. These companies were to garrison fixed fortifications, thereby releasing regular soldiers for active service. This had a direct influence on life in the Royal Hospital, for initially the In-Pensioners were conceived as a garrison with the Hospital as their citadel. Their duty was to guard it and – when required – the roads round about (especially those into central London) and other key locations and buildings. Their enemy would, quite simply, be the King's enemies and, most probably, the London mob which it was feared could rise at a time of national distress or emergency.

To permit the Pensioners to fulfil their military duties to the best of their abilities Ingram saw to the purchase in the 1680s of 369 'fusees' (or fusils, a type of flintlock musket, shorter and lighter than those issued to ordinary infantrymen), twenty-six officers' pikes, thirty-two halberts and sixteen drums. He also organized a body of Pensioners into a guard to stand sentinel at the construction site of the Royal Hospital for its 'better preservation'.

Lieutenant-Governor

'THE ROYAL HOSPITAL IS SOMETHING OF an enigma. If you ask a taxi to take you to the Chelsea Hospital, it will deposit you outside the Chelsea & Westminster Hospital in the Fulham Road. So you must make it clear that you are visiting the home of the Chelsea Pensioners and not a hospital,' says Major-General Jonathan Hall CB OBE, the Lieutenant-Governor.

He is a man who clearly loves the job. His responsibilities are, essentially, the day-to-day running of the Royal Hospital, concentrating on the 'human side' and dealing with the overall care and well-being of the In-Pensioners and staff who work and live there. The job goes back over 300 years but in the last five to ten years the place and working practices have changed tremendously. 'When I came here in 1997 the Royal Hospital was a closed world; it was like walking into a time capsule. It was a place which set its own agenda and pace.'

The Lieutenant-Governor is keen to show people what the Royal Hospital is all about. With his passion to share the Hospital with the world at large, he is deeply – almost romantically – committed to the Pensioners. It is apparent that he cares for them – as one soldier for another – and feels honoured to be of service to men who have done much – and suffered much – for their country in time of war. He talks of them with respect and affection and is amused by their various eccentricities. 'It can be a bit like Peyton Place living here, as everybody knows everybody else's business. I suppose it is bound to be in such a closed environment. The Pensioners are wonderful and tell moving stories. Some of them are straight out of a Victorian music hall, with their shaggy-dog reminiscences.'

As he sees it, the immediate job of the Lieutenant-Governor is to ensure the future of the Royal Hospital by demonstrating that there is a need for such an institution – and the commitments of the British Army, including the war in the Gulf and more recently in Iraq, suggested very dramatically that this is still the case. He says, 'Our mission statement is still current although it was written 300 years ago. We are still achieving the same aim and are determined to continue to do so for the foreseeable future. The fact that the Royal Hospital continues to provide for veteran soldiers, with relatively few physical changes, is a great compliment to Wren's thinking and inspiration'.

The In-Pensioners were regulated and disciplined as would be the garrison of a defended town. 'Taptoo' was sounded at 9pm, a roll-call was taken in each ward and the gates closed at 10pm with guards posted. Pensioners returning late without reason or excuse were confined to a guard room for the night. Furloughs were necessary for travel and restricted to two months. The punishment for most offences was confinement to barracks, but for more serious crimes – such as theft or the illicit selling of Hospital property or new items of uniform – was expulsion from the Royal Hospital and suspension or cancellation of pension.

The organization and running of the Royal Hospital was overseen by its Commissioners – constituted the Chelsea Board in 1703 under the chairmanship of the Paymaster-General (who was also the Hospital Treasurer). Certain officials from the Hospital – such as the Governor and Lieutenant-Governor – were on the Board, but it gradually expanded to include representatives from the Treasury, Government and military departments, as well as military officers.

Initially, however, the Commissioners were Ranelagh, Fox and Wren, who in June 1692 issued detailed instructions to members of staff. The instructions are characterized by a tendency to make the duties of the various officials overlap. This was a formula calculated to cause confusion and friction but which was also a necessary precaution

RIGHT: *Portrait of Sir Thomas Ogle as a young man, from the studio of Gerrit Hontorst. Before obtaining a commission in the Army and his appointment to the Royal Hospital, Ogle had had a mixed career. Imprisoned during the Civil War, he subsequently fell from royal favour by indecently exposing himself on the balcony of a tavern.*

BELOW: *Carved coat of arms on the tomb in the Burial Ground of the first Governor of the Royal Hospital, Lieutenant-Colonel Sir Thomas Ogle, and a detail of the inscription. On the other side the inscription reads, 'Utricia Ashley, late housekeeper of this Hospital. Died April 3 1749. Aged 94 years, at whose charge this Tomb was erected'.*

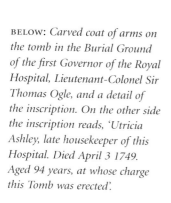

against the spirit of corruption that was a fact of life in late seventeenth-century England. The theory was that each member of staff had the right to monitor and check aspects of the duties of his fellows so that no one had absolute authority over key functions of the Hospital. For example, the Comptroller and the Steward were both required independently to keep an account of the provisions supplied by contract.

The main posts reveal the priorities within the Royal Hospital as perceived by the first Commissioners. The structure was based on that of any great household or college, but with a distinct military and political flavour. The head of the household – the Governor – had the role of both regimental commander and commandant of a garrison. Consequently all Governors have been military men and appointed by the Crown and so, in the early days at least, had a potentially political role to play in state affairs. The

ABOVE: *Tombstone of the Sixpennyman John Carley, his wife and Mrs Mary Codd. Sixpennymen were non-commissioned officers who filled the post of Ward Captain at the Hospital. Thousands of Pensioners and staff were buried in the Burial Ground before it was closed in 1854 and only a few have marked graves.*

first Governor, Sir Thomas Ogle, was a lieutenant-colonel, and when he died in 1702 he was replaced by Colonel John Hales.

The posts below the Governor were filled by half-pay officers or veteran officers resident in the Royal Hospital. The second in command was the man with responsibility for the day-to-day running of the place and the post demanded a certain amount of experimentation. In 1690 there was a Deputy Governor but he was replaced in 1692 by a Lieutenant-Governor, who in 1887 subsumed the position of the Secretary – a post dating from 1688 – supported by an Assistant Secretary. (The post of Secretary was again made independent of that of the Lieutenant-Governor in 2001.) The third in command was the Major – a role that was defined by the energetic and intelligent Captain Matthew Ingram who was the Royal Hospital's first Major, then its first Lieutenant-Governor until his death in March 1694. The post of Major lasted until the mid-nineteenth century. Below the Major was the Adjutant – a post generally filled by officers of relatively junior rank. This was a demanding job and in the early nineteenth century an Assistant Adjutant was appointed; then – in 1834 – it was replaced by a new post called 'Captain of Invalids'.

At first officers had been in charge of each company of In-Pensioners but after 1719, when arrangements started to be made for aged or maimed officers that effectively removed them from Chelsea, the duty of Ward Captain gradually passed to senior NCOs (usually Light Horsemen). By the late eighteenth century these were known as 'Sixpenny-men' because of their slightly higher daily rate of pay.

These pretend officers and 'acting gentlemen' were, predictably, mocked by their genteel neighbours at the Hospital who witnessed their antics in the ale houses: 'The Captains, altho' not one had ever had a captain's commission . . . if you had taken [them] sometimes by the heels . . . and shook them for an hour, you could not have shaken a half crown out of either of their pockets. Yet they frequently had more gold and silver on their clothes than in them'.

In addition to the posts filled by officers and senior NCOs there were also positions that were given largely to civilians. There was the Secretary and Register (until 1887 when the role of Secretary was taken on by the Lieutenant-Governor); the Chaplain (and until 1798 a Second Chaplain); the Organist (a post filled by the distinguished

BELOW: *Pen-and-ink drawing of c. 1800 by John Claude Nattes showing the porch to Dr Burney's apartments designed by Robert Adam and the sash windows that, as Clerk of Works, Adam ordered to replace the earlier mullion windows. The building was destroyed by bombs.*

OPPOSITE: *Pewter plates and leather jacks used in the Great Hall. The jacks were used to carry beer from the cellars beneath the Chapel and the Hall up to the Hall. The brewer was required to keep at least six weeks' supply – or 300 barrels – on the premises. Each jack had a capacity of 5 gallons and cost 11s. in 1699.*

musician and music historian Dr Charles Burney from 1783 to 1814 and Charles Wesley from 1814 to 1817); the Physician and the Surgeon (the post combined in 1832); the Apothecary (until 1816); the Surgeon's Mate, renamed in 1809 the Deputy Surgeon; the Surgeon's Deputy (later renamed Assistant Surgeon and then, in 1816, the Dispenser); the Deputy-Treasurer (until 1836 when the office was abolished); the Comptroller (until 1833 when the office was abolished); the Steward (whose duties since 1855 have been handled by the Quartermaster); and the Clerk of Works whose job it was to maintain the buildings and design and supervise the construction of new accommodation.

Clerk of Works was a valuable and prestigious appointment that was held by a number of leading architects including, from 1765 until 1792, Robert Adam (who replaced virtually all the Royal Hospital's casement windows with sashes and added a number of internal details including the fine Neo-classical mantelpiece in the Governor's Parlour);

RIGHT: *Mantelpiece designed by Robert Adam from the old Pay Office on the south side of Light Horse Court and now the residence of the Secretary.*

Samuel Wyatt from 1792 until 1807; and then Sir John Soane from 1807 until 1837 when the post was abolished. Over the next 155 years the Office and Ministry of Works, then the Ministry of Public Buildings and Works, looked after the property and in 1993 the post of Surveyor of Works was established.

The organization of the Royal Hospital also included a number of minor posts. Among these were the Whitser, in charge of washing the linen (and for whom Wren designed a special laundry); the Wardrobe-keeper, who was responsible for the contents of the building and 'to wait upon all Persons of Quality who wish to see the hospital, and show them the Halls, Wards, Chapel, Walks, etc.'; a Yeoman of the Coal Yards (whose duties were shadowed by the watchful Wardrobe-keeper), the Matron or Housekeeper – the most senior female staff member and – of course – the Master Cook. The role of the Master Cook, and his culinary companions, is well described by Captain Dean, who was a Captain of Invalids and Adjutant of the Royal Hospital during the 1940s, quoting from the Royal Hospital Book of Instructions of 1692.

> The catering arrangements were carefully worked out, and the rations exceptionally generous. Each pensioner was allowed 12 oz. of meat daily, except on Fridays, when fish to the same value was supplied. Also two loaves of bread, ¼ lb. of cheese, two quarts of beer, and unspecified quantities of oatmeal and vegetables. Sergeants and above received an additional 4 oz. of meat. The Steward inspected and kept an account of the provisions supplied by contract, and bought such extra supplies as might be necessary . . .
>
> It was also his duty to visit the kitchens, the dining-halls, before and during meals, and the wards 'to see that they are kept clean and sweet'. As to the Master Cook, he was instructed to keep a careful check on the quality and quantity of the provisions and also that 'You are every day betweene Eleven and Twelve a Clock, when the Drum beats, to begin to Dish the said Meat, Delivering out first the Dishes for the Five Tables in the

Chef

'SOME OF THE PENSIONERS GET upset because they have no family, but we tell them, "don't be upset, we are your family, we are here for life",' confides Zineb Gharbaoui, who has been a chef at the Royal Hospital for thirty years doing the job of the original Master Cook. For her, like most of the staff at the Royal Hospital, her work is more than just a job. In recent years the Royal Hospital's medical staff have given thought to the food on offer in an attempt to get the Pensioners – used to robust Army food – to choose a healthy diet. Low-fat and low-cholesterol dishes are marked on the menu. So what are the Pensioners' favourite dishes – salads and vegetables? Zineb smiles, 'steak and kidney pie, sausage rolls, scotch eggs and sponge and custard'. Clearly old soldiers' bad habits die hard.

Officers Hall, next those for the Sixteen Tables below the Steppe in the Great Hall, Next those for the Governours Table upon the Steppe, And lastly those for the Housekeepers Hall and the Servants Hall, which are not to be served up till one a Clock'.

The serving of meals was supervised by the Master Butler. He was ordered, according to the Instructions,

to take care of all the Plate, etc., belonging to the Governor's Table, to lay the Cloths in the Halls, and to see the Tables properly covered; to take charge of all the pewter thereunto belonging; to take care the Bakers lay the Bread, and that the Butter is brought upon the proper days, and the Mustard upon the Beef days.

The four dining halls were looked after by the Usher of the Hall, who was required to sweep them daily, attend to the fires, clean the tables, open the windows and extinguish the candles.

The dining halls additional to the Great Hall were the Officers' Hall, the Housekeeper's Hall and the Servants' Hall. The Officers' Hall (for Light Horse Pensioners as well as officers) was located in the north-west wing. Its function changed in 1740 when the Governor swapped dining accommodation with the officers: he moved into their hall and they moved onto tables in the Great Hall. But by 1797 the Gentlemen's Hall (as it was called) had become the Board Room, was then allocated for use by NCOs, and finally became the Billiard Room in 1946. The Housekeeper's Hall (for use by upper servants) was closed in 1740 but used for festivals until 1846. From 1797 its general use was as a waiting room. It is now the Adjutant's Office and television room. The Servants' Hall was abolished in 1740 but continued to be used by Matrons (nurses) until the end of the eighteenth century.

The original dining regime in the Hospital is made most clear in the Instructions. The Pensioners were well fed on meat, fish, vegetables, bread and cheese, and well supplied with beer. They sat on benches attached to the sixteen tables with iron bars and the tables were covered with cloths. These tablecloths would – as was the custom of the time – have reached to the floor and doubled up as napkins. Differences of rank were acknowledged in the quantity (if not the quality) of the food served and the order in which the diners were served as well as the places where they sat. Clearly not all the In-Pensioners could be fed at one sitting, although probably the overflow

Dining-Hall Waitress

WHEN PAT IGBANUGO FIRST arrived for work in the Great Hall – taking the Pensioners' orders and serving their food – she was shocked to see so many men. 'I felt they were all like my father.' Twenty-three years later, just as she is about to retire, the roles have been reversed and Pat has become a familiar mother-figure for them. She is ready to render moral support and advice along with the food, especially to newcomers who feel homesick and lonely, and find it difficult to fit into the established community. 'I love the names they give you – "petal", "flower" – it makes you feel happy.'

Chaplain

RICHARD WHITTINGTON MBE – inevitably called Dick – became Chaplain to the Royal Hospital early in 2001. He joined the Army as a boy soldier and, after twenty-nine years' service, had risen to the rank of colonel. But then came a dramatic change of direction. He left the Army, read theology and was ordained in 1993. He became a parish priest until, because of his military background, he was invited to apply for the job at Chelsea. In the meantime, in 1998, he was appointed a Gentleman at Arms, one of the Queen's ceremonial bodyguards. Having been commissioned from the ranks, Whittington feels a particular empathy with the In-Pensioners; he knows the world from which many of them come.

The Chaplain has two distinct jobs.

First there is the pastoral work with the Pensioners, including conducting a funeral a week, on average. Second there is the administrative and managerial side. The Chapel is a fashionable London church, open to the public, with a fine professional choir and some very distinguished regular worshippers, so the Chaplain has certain social and parochial obligations. But, as Whittington emphasizes, 'what's really important is working with the Pensioners'. His relationship with them can become very close – and transcends denominational boundaries: 'Just now one of the gentlemen stopped me and said, "Padre, on paper I'm Roman Catholic, but will you take my funeral?"'

Whittington relishes working in one of the finest churches in London but chooses to describe aspects of it as 'awful'. The Chapel is, he says, 'in some respects, everything you wouldn't want – it breaks every rule for addressing those who are hard of hearing. You should be face to face with your congregation but the collegiate seating means one half of the congregation faces the other. And the pulpit is too high. At all times one is talking to the backs or sides of the heads of at least half the congregation'. Worse, in his view, is the fact that the Chapel – like the Great Hall – is raised high above ground level. The steep steps can prove difficult for many of the In-Pensioners although ascending to the Chapel feels and looks good. But he approves of the decoration of the Chapel interior – 'very good, understated Wren'.

was accommodated in other ways with, no doubt, a fair number being regularly indisposed or confined to the Infirmary.

The impressive size of the Great Hall and the great mural painting by Verrio on the end wall, together with the intrinsic interest of its antiquated occupants and the rituals surrounding the serving of dinner, soon made meal times at Chelsea one of the popular sights of London. This interest was anticipated from the start and an instruction of 1692 ordered the Usher 'not to suffer strangers to come into the Hall when the Pensioners are at dinner, but if they desire to see them eat to admit them in the Gallery'.

An order in the Adjutant's Journal of 1769 gives some idea of what visitors would have seen. The drums would beat in Figure Court at around twelve noon and the red-clad veterans would gather and then troop into the Hall. The men would assemble around their respective tables and the 'Serjeants' – obliged to 'daily attend in the Hall at Dinner and Supper Time' – would 'gravely say Grace at the Head of their Tables' and ensure that 'the men at their respective Tables behave with Order, Silence and Decency.'

Dinners were probably far livelier than this description might imply. However, religious discipline was built firmly into the life of the Hospital. Attendance at Chapel was compulsory. There was a bench for each ward – organized in collegiate fashion as if the Pensioners were monks – with box pews for staff and officers and benches in the gallery for female staff. There were two services a day and a Sunday church parade, and

RIGHT: *Carol Service in the Chapel of the Royal Hospital, open to visitors, as are all the services. The services were originally held twice daily and Pensioners and staff were obliged to attend. They were announced by the Sexton who walked from the London Gate to the Chelsea Gate ringing a hand-bell, and while they were in progress the Porter was stationed in the Porch to ensure that 'the congregation may not be disturbed by idle persons or Dogs'. The Pensioners attended Chapel independently, except on Sunday mornings when they marched there under the Sergeant of their ward.*

OPPOSITE: *The large pair of altar candlesticks were probably made to Wren's own specification. The maker's mark, 'R L', which is found on most of the silver-gilt pieces, including the alms dish with the cypher of James II, is believed to be that of Ralph Leete, who made the plate for St James's, Piccadilly, and for the church probably built by Wren at Farley, Wiltshire, for Sir Stephen Fox. The altar cross was designed in 1954 by Leslie Durbin to match the candlesticks.*

visitors regularly joined the old soldiers. Indeed the Chapel was more than just a curiosity of west London for, from its consecration in 1691, it became a popular place for baptisms and marriages. It was also used initially for the funerals of Pensioners, who were buried – until 1854 in the Hospital Burial Ground – with full military honours.

IV
GEORGIAN CHELSEA

ABOVE: *View of the Royal Hospital by Edward Haytley, c. 1746. The picture belongs to the Foundling Hospital, another of London's charitable foundations. It was set up by a Royal Charter of 1739 for the 'Maintenance and Education of Exposed and Deserted Young Children' by the philanthropist Sir Thomas Coram.*

PREVIOUS PAGE: *Early eighteenth-century view of Chelsea and the Royal Hospital from the south bank of the Thames, an oil painting by Peter Tillemans. Much of London's traffic was water-borne at this period, affording passengers a fine view of Wren's building and the pair of cubical waterside pavilions and the octagonal summer house built for Sir Robert Walpole.*

W HEN THE FIRST PENSIONERS arrived at Chelsea during the 1690s the Royal Hospital stood in countryside, adjoined only by the small riverside village of Chelsea with its ancient church and a scattering of mansions along the banks of the Thames. Soon terraces of speculatively built houses arose along the south end of Church Street and to each side of the church itself. In the surrounding area there was a terrace along the north side of Paradise Row, immediately to the west of the Hospital, a scattering of villas and a few houses and inns on – or near – King's Road and other ancient thoroughfares.

Gradually, during the eighteenth century, Chelsea was engulfed by a wave of terrace houses and became part of the great and sprawling metropolis. It started with the coherent development of Cheyne Walk, Cheyne Row and Jews Row in about 1703. By 1820 King's Road was still not fully lined with terraces but there were groups of buildings closely spaced along its east end, while Smith Street – linking King's Road with the Royal Hospital – had acquired a very urban aspect. Royal Avenue (then called White Stiles) had only a terrace of ten houses at its south-west corner. Facing towards Royal Avenue was the Royal Military Asylum, subsequently named the Duke of York's Headquarters. Built in 1801–3, it had been designed by John Sanders in grandiose manner to compete with its illustrious neighbour.

One of the key reasons for this development of Chelsea was, undoubtedly, the Royal Hospital. It was a noble urban ornament closely connected with the monarchy and also its community of armed and disciplined veterans ensured tranquillity from housebreakers and the mob. In addition, the Chelsea Pensioners were, in themselves, a powerful economic force. In-Pensioners were steady customers at local inns and many a local boarding-house thrived on the business generated by the fact that old soldiers had, until 1845, to apply in person for admission to the Royal Hospital and even to claim a pension.

Jews Row, opposite the Burial Ground, became famed for its inns – much used by the In-Pensioners – and for its brothels. By the early nineteenth century the gardens between Jews Row and Turks Row to its north had been turned into a series of narrow courts lined with low houses. In 1823 the area was described as a 'swarm of stews ... the resort of Israelites, Prostitutes and Publicans' and it was soon afterwards condemned by Thomas

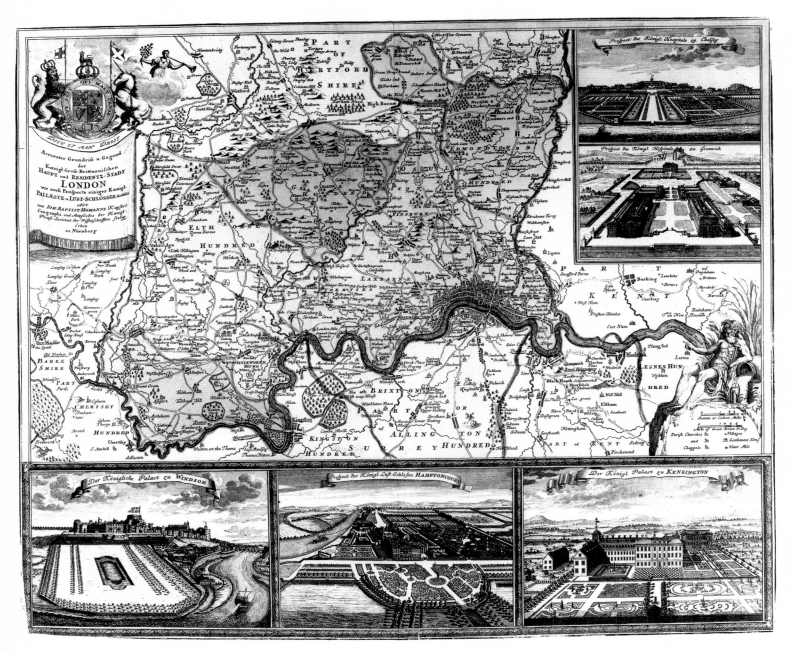

ABOVE: *Map of London and its environs published by Homann and dating from c. 1710. The inset engravings are of the three principal royal palaces: Windsor Castle, Hampton Court and Kensington Palace. The inclusion of Chelsea Hospital and Greenwich Hospital demonstrates their contemporary importance.*

RIGHT: *Portrait of Richard Jones, 3rd Earl of Ranelagh (1641–1712), from the studio of Sir Peter Lely. Ranelagh was described as 'a man of good parts, great wit, and very little religion; had an head turned for projects, and was formed for intrigue, artful, insinuating, and designing, craving and greedy of money, yet at the same time profuse and lavish'. He was Paymaster-General and Treasurer of the Hospital from 1685 to 1702.*

Faulkner – a Chelsea historian – as a disgrace to the parish. This state of affairs is hardly surprising. By no means all the inhabitants of the Royal Hospital were old or terminally infirm and many had contrived to create – on their doorstep – the type of licentious nether-world that tended to grow up within the environs of most British barracks.

Within the grounds of the Royal Hospital the principal changes that took place during the eighteenth century were in some way connected with Lord Ranelagh. Having acquired a lease on the house that he had had built as the official residence of the Treasurer – and considerably embellished using funds intended for the main building –

BELOW: *Nineteenth-century watercolour of Walpole's 1720s garden pavilion on an angle of the Thames at Coal Creek. The columned porch was an addition. The gilded pineapple crowning the ogival domed roof was a landmark on Chelsea Reach until the building's demolition around 1872.*

Ranelagh contrived to keep it as his own property when he resigned the position. This situation soon became highly inconvenient to the Hospital.

When John Howe became Paymaster-General – and consequently Treasurer – in December 1702 he had to be allocated modest lodgings in one corner of the stables that Wren had built to the west of the Hospital. These were taken over by Sir Robert Walpole (later Lord Orford) when he became Paymaster-General in October 1714 – a position he held for only a year but which he regained – again for only a year – in 1720.

Notwithstanding his brief tenure as Paymaster-General and Treasurer, Walpole obtained a thirty-one-year lease on the property (paying a nominal rent of £10 a year) and made extensive alterations and additions to his official lodgings (no doubt at Hospital expense). These included a garden pavilion and a brick-built and large-windowed Orangery facing south towards the river (and now containing the Royal Hospital's Library).

The architect for the alterations and additions that Walpole carried out in 1715–16 was Sir John Vanbrugh. He had been Comptroller of the Office of Works since 1702, was a colleague of Wren and a close supporter of Walpole who, along with the Duke of Marlborough (for whom Vanbrugh had designed Blenheim Palace, Oxfordshire), managed to secure Vanbrugh's knighthood in 1714. Thus another slice of Royal Hospital property was alienated, through unscrupulous manoeuvering by officers only too happy to abuse their privileged position.

The property passed through various hands – the lease being extended – until 1804 when it was inherited by Lord Yarborough. He, in 1808, disposed of the lease to the Treasury, which shortly afterwards transferred it to the Royal Hospital for use as a much-needed Infirmary.

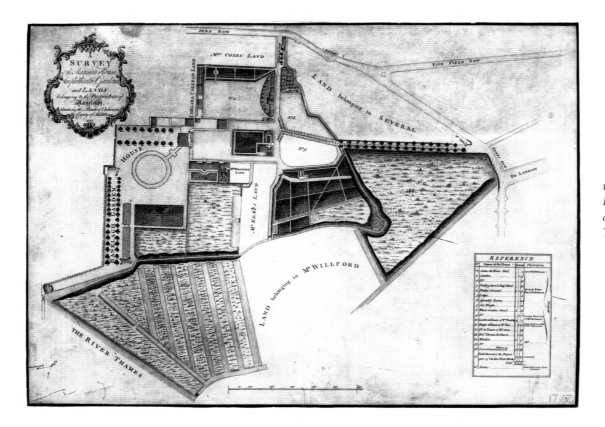

LEFT: *Map of 1777 of the Ranelagh estate land that was developed as pleasure grounds. The Rotunda is shown at the left.*

ABOVE: *The changed view of the Royal Hospital from the river in an eighteenth-century painting, with the Rotunda visible on the right. The building was 150 feet (46m.) in diameter. After falling attendance, it was demolished in 1805.*

More significant than Vanbrugh's relatively modest works to the west of the Hospital was the development that overtook the land that had been leased in the 1680s to Ranelagh. Located immediately to the east of the Hospital, this parcel of land had been transformed by Ranelagh into a handsome miniature estate with mansion house, stables, dovecotes and varied ornamental and utilitarian buildings.

The roguish Ranelagh eventually fell upon hard times but, at his death in 1712, the estate was still in his possession. His daughter, Lady Catherine Jones, was in occupation and despite her father's dire debts she managed to hang on to the estate until 1730. At this time she vested the estate in trustees and three years later it was divided into ten lots and put up for auction. Eventually the Hospital purchased a three-acre plot to add

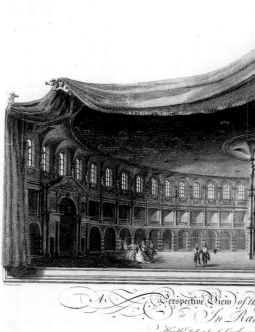

ABOVE: 'By His Majesty's Command The Jubilee Ball after the Venetian manner, Or Masquerade at Ranelagh Gardens April the 26th 1749'. The legend reads, 'England most fond of Foreign Follies grown, each new Device adopts, and makes her own ... From Venice they import the Fresco Ball, Where Nymphs in loose and Antick Robes appear, And motley shapes our Warlike Heroes wear'. Engraving after a drawing by Louis Philippe Boitard.

to its gardens, but most of the estate was acquired by speculators who hoped to find ways around restrictions in the Crown lease on the land that prohibited 'incommodious' new buildings near the Hospital.

By 1737 a prominent west London speculative builder, Benjamin Timbrell, had acquired Ranelagh House and erected one new house near it. Four years later Timbrell was part of a business syndicate – led by Mr Lacey, co-patentee of the Drury Lane Theatre, and including a Member of Parliament called Sir Thomas Robinson – that resolved to turn the property into a pleasure ground. This was a controversial scheme that clearly threatened to disturb the peace of the Pensioners – and matters were made worse because the scheme involved the construction of a huge rotunda in which revelers could dine, dance, parade and listen to music. Such a construction – 185 feet (56m.) in diameter – could without doubt be construed as 'incommodious' to the Hospital buildings that would undeniably be upstaged by such an ostentatious construction.

While the Hospital authorities looked on in surprise the syndicate – with a haste that was little short of sheer impudence – quickly raised the massive amphitheatre-like structure. The builder was Timbrell and the designer was William Jones – surveyor to the East India Company.

The Royal Hospital eventually objected to the construction of the Rotunda and did – legally – have the power under the Crown lease to stop the works or even to have the

ABOVE: *Engraved view of the interior of the Rotunda published by William Newton in 1761. Booths for drinking tea and wine can be seen around the walls.*

ABOVE RIGHT: *'The Chinese House, the Rotunda and the Company in Masquerade', an engraving dating from the mid-1760s. The chinoiserie pavilion in the ornamental lake was built in 1750. The anonymity afforded by the masks released the wearer from normal codes of behaviour.*

Rotunda torn down. But the complaints were lame in the extreme and not sustained. In the end the Hospital Commissioners caved in and agreed disadvantageous terms with the syndicate and the project continued.

This strange affair is one of the mysteries in the history of the Royal Hospital. It can only be assumed that – in the manner of the unscrupulous Lord Ranelagh – someone in a position of power in the Hospital had something personal to gain by the development of the Rotunda and pleasure grounds. The finger of blame points towards Henry Pelham – who was Paymaster-General and Hospital Treasurer from May 1730 until December 1743 – and at the Governor during the critical period in the 1730s, Major-General William Evans. It is hard to imagine how the Governor could, without the support of the Treasurer, manipulate the Hospital to agree to such a deal. The next Governor, Lieutenant-General Sir Robert Rich, was unable or unwilling to do anything and the Rotunda and pleasure grounds duly opened in April 1742.

Despite the unscrupulous way in which the Rotunda was erected – and its failure to relate in any way to the geometry, scale or architecture of Wren's Hospital buildings – it was a fascinating, bold and pioneering structure that in many respects anticipated nineteenth-century places of public resort. Its huge roof (famous at the time as an ingenious piece of timber construction) had only one interior support – a central colonnaded pier of complex form that also served as a stack for a massive fireplace.

REGATTA BALL AT RANELAGH

ABOVE: *Ticket for the Regatta Ball, 28th June 1775, the Rotunda in the background. Engraved by F. Bartolozzi after a drawing by G. B. Cipriani.*

Around the walls of the Rotunda was a deep arcade supporting boxes that were used by diners with – on one side – a large ornamental stand for the orchestra. Outside were tree-lined walks, pavilions, a canal and, to the north, Ranelagh House that was connected to the Rotunda by an arcade.

As soon as they opened the Ranelagh pleasure grounds became one of the most famous sights in London and was quickly more popular than the well-established Vauxhall pleasure gardens, just across the river. They were the epitome of mid-eighteenth-century London life. At Ranelagh high life and low life, aristocrats and rogues, artists and harlots met and mixed, their different lives overlapping and interpenetrating. Mozart performed in the Rotunda, Canaletto painted it, George II was a regular visitor, Horace Walpole, soon after the gardens opened, recorded that 'It has totally beat Vauxhall . . . You can't set your foot without treading on a Prince, or Duke of Cumberland'. On the other hand Edward Gibbon thought it 'the most convenient place for courtships of every kind – the best market we have in England'.

Despite its popularity and high ticket prices – on firework nights the charge could be as high as 5s. – the enterprise failed to flourish. The syndicate faced bankruptcy, but was saved by Robinson who became the principal shareholder and built, just to the east of the Rotunda, a sedate house that he occupied until his death in 1777. Thereafter the enterprise gradually went downhill. In 1803 the gardens closed and two years later the Rotunda, pavilions and Lord Ranelagh's fine 1680s mansion were all pulled down. The setting of the Royal Hospital was restored and tranquillity returned.

The precedent set by Lord Ranelagh for shameless abuse of office, combined with the frivolous atmosphere of the neighbouring Ranelagh Gardens, seems to have had a very debilitating effect on the Royal Hospital. The mid to late eighteenth century became a period characterized by casual corruption and mismanagement when the essential aim of the institution – the provision of accommodation, care and dignified retirement for a select band of old soldiers – was gradually obscured by other concerns. The Royal Hospital – or rather its funds and the employments it offered – were purloined and abused as a matter of course.

It became common to turn positions into mere sinecures by awarding them to people who were absentees or utterly unsuitable for the position. Many of the subordinate posts

Epitaph, on the late D.ʳ Monsey, supposed to be written by himself.

Here lie my old limbs — my vexation now ends,
for I've lived much, too long for myself & my Friends,
As to church yards & grounds which the Parsons call holy,
'Tis a rank piece of priestcraft & founded on folly:

In short, I despise them: and as for my Soul,
Which may mount the last day with my bones from this hole,
I think that it really hath nothing to fear
From the God of mankind, whom I truly revere.

What the next world may be, little troubles my pate
If not better than this, I beseech thee, Oh! Fate,
When the bodies of millions fly up in a riot,
To let the old carcase of Monsey lie quiet.

Peter Pindar

Pub.ᵈ Jan.ʸ 19.ᵗʰ 1789, by H. Humphrey, New Bond S.ᵗ

LEFT: *Satirical print, published in 1789, on the death of Dr Monsey at the age of ninety-five. He had been Physician at the Hospital for forty-seven years. Entitled 'Ornaments of Chelsea Hospital, – or – a peep into the last Century', it includes an epitaph, supposedly written by himself, which includes the words, 'What the next world may be, little troubles my pate If not better than this, I beseech thee, Oh Fate, When the bodies of millions fly up in a riot, To let the old carcase of Monsey lie quiet'.*

were filled by widows of former officials and in 1786 Francis Grose, a sharp observer of London life, commented with heavy irony that, 'it is a melancholy consideration that of the many superannuated quarter masters, serjeant-majors and serjeants in and about the Hospital, none can be found worthy to fill up the inferior offices of the house'. This was, thought Grose, a strange state of affairs since it was these able men who 'are in great measure the nerves and sinews of our armies, who bear the brunt of the battles, and the fatigue of the day [and] to rob them of their right in this charity is peculiarly cruel'. Dr Messenger Monsey, appointed Physician to the Royal Hospital in 1742 and one of the more engaging eccentrics of eighteenth-century London with a reputation for straight-talking, pulled no punches in his memoirs, published posthumously in 1789: 'the College at Chelsea, which ought to have been devoted to national charity, was over-run by valets, grooms or election-jobbers . . . By this preposterous misapplication of public rewards, a man, by shaving the Paymaster, brushing his coat, his shoes, or marrying his mistress, became the companion of a General, a knight of the Bath, a Physician and a Divine'.

Organist

'IT'S A WONDERFUL LIFE AND A privilege to live here,' says Ian Curror, who has been Organist at the Royal Hospital since 1974 and lives in a splendid apartment originally designed by Soane for the Surgeon. It is a job that goes back to the foundation of the Royal Hospital and has been filled by some eminent musicians indeed – notably Dr Charles Burney, a friend of Haydn who stayed with him in the Royal Hospital.

Originally services were held in the Chapel twice a day. Now there is only a Sunday service, a number of special services and three or four weddings a year, so the Organist has the freedom to develop other musical interests, including performance, teaching and composition. What has increased in importance is the Choir. In the early days the Choir was formed by local schoolchildren, but now it is a professional choir, with its members paid by the Royal Hospital and operating under the musical direction of the Organist.

Ian reflects on the changing nature of music – both that played in the Royal Hospital Chapel and generally. 'We're all members of the "Dead Musicians Society" – in the main we play music written by people now dead. But Burney would have played music by contemporary musicians – by people very much alive, or only recently dead like Handel.' Ian tries to recapture this spirit – the excitement that comes from contemporary or experimental music. 'It is very important our congregation hears music – new as well as old – as a background to the service from the 1662 Book of Common Prayer.' Do the Pensioners enjoy the occasional mix of new and old? Ian believes so and is sure that – given the frank nature of old soldiers – he would know all about it if they did not.

Dr Charles Burney was an eminent musicologist, but the way in which in 1783 he secured the post of Organist at the Royal Hospital – through a mixture of political and social manoeuvering – was typical of the way in which such sinecures were awarded at the time. Burney's daughter, Fanny, described the way in which Edmund Burke – family friend, politician and briefly Paymaster-General of the Royal Hospital – put the offer to her father in 1783.

Mr Burke, 'feeling his way, by the most investigating looks, as he proceeded said that the organist's place at Chelsea College was vacant: that it was but 20 pounds a year, but that, to a man of Dr. Burney's eminence, if it should be worth acceptance, it might be raised to fifty ... Trifling as this was in a pecuniary light, and certainly far beneath the age or the rank in his profession of Dr. Burney, to possess any thing through the influence, or rather the friendship of Mr. Burke, had a charm inestimable. The Doctor wished, also, for some retreat from, yet near London; and he had reason to hope for apartments, ere long, in the capacious Chelsea College'.

Burke was soon to ask a favour in return – Burney's support for a protégé during a Westminster election – but Burney's political conscience would not permit him to aid his patron. To both men's credit, letters of extreme politeness were exchanged over the matter and there was no breach in their friendship. By 1786 or 1787 Burney was in possession of his apartment, that officially allocated to the Chaplain.

In 1798 the Chaplain desired the use of his official accommodation and this presented Burney – and the Royal Hospital – with a tricky problem. Burney, through his social connections and musical reputation had, without doubt, given the Royal Hospital a certain lustre. Through him people of eminence and influence had come to visit the Royal Hospital and attend services in the Chapel. For example Joseph Haydn, a friend and admirer of Burney had, during his two London visits of 1791–92 and 1794–95, stayed in Burney's apartment. But the Chelsea Board was obliged to follow its own rules. So Burney had to suffer the indignity of being turned out of his home. To make amends another apartment was found but this, allocated to the Second Chaplain, was smaller than Burney's former home – and he had to pay rent. It was in this small apartment – on the second floor of the main building and subsequently damaged by wartime bombing – that Burney lived until his death in 1814.

SIR CECILS BUDGET FOR PAYING THE NATIONAL DEBT

Pub. March 30. 1784 by M.ᵉ Dacheray S.ᵗ James's Street

The organization of the Governor's dining arrangements during this period is emblematic of the attitudes that prevailed. By the second half of the eighteenth century the medieval tradition of the highest and lowest dining together in the Great Hall had been broken, and the Governor was presiding over what was virtually a private dining club in the Gentlemen's Hall. Lavish amounts of food and wine were provided at public expense for a variety of fashionable guests – often with no particular connection to the Royal Hospital or its function. The Governor and his clique settled themselves, in polite and intimate harmony and comfort, in fourteen fashionable upholstered chairs (costing 15 guineas – or six months' salary for an ordinary working man in mid-eighteenth-century London).

Invitations to dinner at the Royal Hospital were much sought after by Londoners and foreign visitors, especially for the two annual Festival Dinners that celebrated Oak Apple Day (commemorating the birthday of Charles II, founder of the Hospital, and also the day of his restoration) and the birthday of the reigning monarch. James Boswell managed to secure an invitation to a Festival Dinner in May 1783, through his friendship with Edmund Burke, who shortly before had been appointed Paymaster-General.

ABOVE: *A proposal was made in 1784 by a member of the Government, Sir Cecil Wray, that the national economy could be improved by closing down the Chelsea Hospital (and giving each In-Pensioner £20 to live where he pleased) and taxing the employers of maidservants. Thomas Rowlandson's satirical print shows desperate Pensioners fleeing a crumbling Hospital while in the background Sir Cecil is roundly beaten up by maids (one of whom is emptying a chamber-pot over his head) and a single Pensioner lets fly with his crutch.*

Boswell's and Burke's host was Sir George Howard, a former commanding officer of the Buffs, and long-serving Member of Parliament who had been Governor of the Royal Hospital for fifteen years. Boswell recorded, 'I sat between Mr. Burke and Dr. Mounsey [*sic*], Physician to the College who in his eighty-ninth year was quite entire in his mind . . . We had an excellent dinner, and a great deal of good wines. I drank liberally'. Sir George Howard asked him to dine there every anniversary as long as he was Governor and Boswell took the Governor's standing invitation seriously, attending Festival Dinners regularly until 1790. That year it seems to have been a particularly lavish affair. 'It was an excellent dinner, as usual, and I drank of all the liquors: cold drink, small beer, ale, porter, cyder, madeira, sherry, old hock, port, Claret . . . I was much intoxicated, and I suppose talked nonsense.'

Things started to change as the eighteenth century came to a close. Complaints were made and in 1796 the Chelsea Board initiated an inquiry. It made alarming discoveries. Despite free fruit and vegetables supplied from the kitchen garden, and excluding bread, the cost of provisions for the Governor's table amounted to £327 per annum – a huge cost, roughly equivalent to the value of the annual pensions of eighteen private soldiers. The consumption of liquor each week consisted of nineteen bottles of Port, three of Claret and six pints of Sherry. The Chelsea Board, abashed by these revelations, immediately abolished the Governor's Table except, until 1846, for the two annual festivals.

The *London Evening Post* of 14th March 1789 describes a special service that reveals the important role played by the Royal Hospital Chapel. To celebrate George III's recovery from his bout of insanity the Royal Hospital organized a service of thanksgiving with Burney performing on the superb organ built by Renatus Harris in 1693 (rebuilt in 1817 and 1934). Children from local charity schools and Sunday schools processed into the Chapel with red-coated In-Pensioners and all the local dignitaries while the organ was 'animated by Dr. Burney'. When the solemn but joyous ceremony was concluded the children were given a good dinner while the In-Pensioners 'rapidly liquidated the sum of £81 that had been distributed amongst them'.

The King's recovery lasted for fifteen years and, just before he lapsed into terminal illness, George III visited the place where his recovery had been celebrated. Dr Burney

ABOVE: *The Duke of Marlborough, in scarlet coat and mounted on a bay charger, leads his troops to victory at the Battle of Blenheim of 1704 in the War of the Spanish Succession. The painting is by John Wootton.*

was present to record the event. The visit – by the King, the Queen and most of the Royal Family with the exception of the Prince of Wales – took place in 1805. As Burney wrote, 'they went over every ward, the Governor's apartment, and all the offices, with the chapel, refectory and even the kitchen. I was graciously summoned when they entered the chapel, and most graciously, indeed, received'.

The Chelsea Pensioners during the eighteenth century would have seen action in many and diverse parts of the world. In the early years of the century a few of the elderly Pensioners would have served during the Civil War, but soon the bulk would have been veterans of Marlborough's army and the Flanders and German campaigns of 1702–13. Then the ranks of Chelsea would have swelled with men who had served during the War of the Austrian Succession and the Jacobite Rebellion; by survivors of the lucky victory at Dettingen in 1743, when George II was the last British monarch to lead an army in the field, and of the bloody and honourable repulse at Fontenoy in 1745; and by witnesses of the ghastly slaughter at Culloden in April 1746, when the English Army under the Duke of Cumberland ended a way of life in the Scottish Highlands. By the late eighteenth century In-Pensioners from these campaigns would have been joined by veterans from the great imperial and dynastic struggle of the age, the Seven Years' War, which raged and flickered around the globe – on land and sea – with major actions fought in Europe, India and in the French and British colonies in North America.

Order of BATTLE of the Confederate ARMY at RAMILLY
His Highness the Prince & Duke of MARLBOROUGH Commander in Chief. His Excellency the Lord AUVERQUERQUE Velt Maresc
Count de TILLY General of the Horse. CHURCHIL General of the Foot.

BATTLE OF RAMILLIES

William Hiseland was one of the In-Pensioners of the Royal Hospital who had served in Flanders with the army of the Duke of Marlborough. This campaign was fought between 1702 and 1713 as part of the War of the Spanish Succession and in many ways to secure and exploit the momentous victory of August 1704 at Blenheim, in Bavaria. It included many sieges and three great battles: Ramillies in May 1706, Oudenarde in July 1708 and Malplaquet in September 1709.

At Ramillies Marlborough was in sole command of an Anglo-Dutch army of 62,000 opposing a French army of 60,000 under the command of Marshal Villeroi. The object of the action was the allied conquest of the Spanish Netherlands. The two armies met on the plain of Ramillies, where the French were already entrenched along a low ridge, with villages and marshes turned into strong points, and with their right flank protected by the River Mehaigne. But despite the apparent strength of this defensive position Marshal Villeroi had, in fact, overextended his forces and this was a fatal flaw that Marlborough, with his forces arriving as a compact unit, noticed immediately. So Marlborough not only possessed the initial advantage enjoyed by the attacker – he was to choose the time and location of the opening action – but also had shorter internal lines of communication so his forces could be moved with greater speed. Also, as luck would have it, the allied force enjoyed the additional advantage of a fold in the land that concealed the transfer of forces from the centre of either flank of the attacking army.

After an hour's bombardment the allied forces attacked both French flanks simultaneously, in response to which Villeroi dispatched forces from his centre, which was thus seriously weakened. Marlborough – playing the battle like a game of chess – had, within an hour of the action opening, grabbed and sustained the initiative and was imposing his will on the enemy. The centre was being softened up for the *coup de grâce*. In desperation, the French cavalry on the right charged and, in a sudden reversal of fortune, the allied cavalry was almost routed. But Marlborough – displaying his skill not only as a lofty tactician but also as a blood-and-guts fighting general – speedily gathered allied cavalry from elsewhere on the field and led the riposte.

During the bitter clash between the cavalry squadrons Marlborough almost paid the ultimate price. As General Orkney recorded, 'Milord Marlborough was rid over, but got other squadrons to his aid which he led up. Major Bingfield, holding his stirrup to give him assistance onto his horse, was shot by a cannon ball that passed through Marlborough's legs'. In fact Bingfield – the Duke's equerry – had his head carried off by a cannon ball, as the horrified Marlborough looked on. The French cavalry was repulsed and the Maison du Roi – the élite Household Cavalry of the French monarchy – was demolished, losing its silver kettle-drums and Negro drummers.

The flank attacks were going well but Marlborough could see that victory would only be achieved if the French centre was broken – and quickly – for the day was drawing to a close. To achieve this he did something that seemed shocking – indeed did shock his commander almost to the point of rebellion. The Duke called off the assault and the troops under Orkney had to retire.

The allied soldiers were then ordered to make a show. Half their number occupied their old positions in a most ostentatious manner, fooling the French into believing that the whole force remained by the simple ruse of leaving the colour-parties of each battalion behind. It seemed the French could not conceive of soldiers fighting without their colours. While this pantomime was underway, the remaining half of the flank force slipped away to reinforce an attacking force gathered in the centre of the allied position. At five in the afternoon the great – and surprise – assault against the weakened French centre was launched. The French broke, Villeroi tried to rally and form a line among his own tents, but this soon crumbled in the confusion of baggage and guy ropes.

WILLIAM HISELAND

In the Royal Hospital there hangs a portrait of William Hiseland dressed in the uniform worn by Chelsea Pensioners in the early eighteenth century. Somewhat at odds with the quizzical smile on his face, this aged warrior is brandishing a heavy sword. The picture was painted in 1730 when the subject was 110 years of age, or so it is claimed in the inscription. He started his military service in 1632 at the age of thirteen and entered the Royal Hospital in 1713 at the age of ninety-three, after giving over eighty years' service to the Crown. He is the first Pensioner of whom there exists a visual record.

ABOVE: *Hand-coloured engraving of 'A View of the Glorious Action of Dettingen, June 1743, between the Forces of the Allies Commanded by the King of Great Britain and the French Army under Marshal Noailles'. The battle was fought during the War of the Austrian Succession.*

The lives of the aged and infirm In-Pensioners were well regulated and military in tone but many of the Pensioners would have been relatively young and able and so capable of a certain amount of active service. Some Pensioners were organized to patrol and watch the roads between Chelsea and Westminster and were expected to form guard parties at times of civil strife. But, of more military significance, was the organization of Pensioners into military units that could act as a Reserve Army when required.

The idea of regarding Chelsea Pensioners as a potential military resource goes back to the early days of the Royal Hospital when, in 1688, James II – just before his overthrow – initiated the formation of Invalid Companies. In 1703 the Board of the Royal Hospital was given the responsibility of regulating these Invalid Companies and, by 1718, it had 4,926 Out-Pensioners on its books. The following year these veterans were organized

into Regiments of Invalids and by the 1760s, due to the heavy recruiting during the War of the Austrian Succession and the Seven Years' War, the Invalid Regiments had grown to eleven in number.

The main duty of the Invalid units was to release regular troops for mobile operations in Britain's growing empire by performing garrison duty in Britain and by manning fixed coastal fortifications against invasion or incursion. This policy came into its own during the Napoleonic Wars when much of Britain's coastal defence against French invasion was in the hands of local, largely untrained, militias organized around units of seasoned veterans. In subtle recognition of this key role the name and structure of the Pensioners' units was changed in 1807. The numerous Regiments of Invalids were replaced by the somewhat more dignified Regiments of Veterans, composed of a number of separate battalions.

During these tumultuous times not all the Chelsea Pensioners were men. Women could have a very tough time in the eighteenth century. If intelligent and independent of spirit, but not well educated or the beneficiary of inherited high status or wealth, a woman had few options. None of the recognized careers was open to women – she could not practise law or medicine – though she could, if possessed of the necessary natural talents and ornaments, try her hand at the arts. This generally meant the stage which was, to the eighteenth-century mind, merely a branch of prostitution. Or, to survive and flourish in a man's world a woman could – quite simply – become a man. She could dress as a man, act as a man and attempt to do a man's work. Naturally enough, this choice involved a certain amount of secrecy and subterfuge, but it appears to have been a career which many women entered and at which many succeeded – at least for a surprisingly long period of time – presumably due to the willingness of male comrades to enter into the conspiracy.

The most dramatic way for a woman to operate in a man's world was to embrace the most masculine career of all, namely to enlist as a soldier. The records of the Royal Hospital include accounts of two women who not only managed to join the British Army in the guise of men – and to remain within its ranks for some considerable time – but who eventually succeeded in becoming Out-Pensioners of the Royal Hospital. There is a powerful myth of the female soldier, recorded and romanticized in numerous eighteenth- and early nineteenth-century ballads, and the usual – and acceptable – explanation offered is that the girl changed her sex for love, to pursue, find or rescue her soldier sweetheart. This veneer is offered to the so-called Chelsea 'Amazons'.

Catherine Walsh or Welch – known also as Mother Ross or Davis – served with the Royal North British Dragoons (the Royal Scots Greys) and in 1717 was awarded a pension of 5d. (later raised to 1s.) for her service in Flanders during Queen Anne's wars. According to a contemporary account her sex was only discovered when she was wounded, at the Battle of Ramillies in May 1706, until which time, 'her Comrade had not the least Suspicion of her being a Woman'.

How can this have been so – given the rough and tumble of military life in the eighteenth century? Or did her companions know the secret but declined to betray the truth to their officers? For whatever reason, Catherine Walsh was clearly a brave woman

Mezzotint of Hannah Snell, one of the Chelsea 'Amazons', which was published in 1750, the year that the story of her extraordinary life in the Army appeared. The print, by John Faber, is after the painting by Richard Phelps. The legend beneath the print relates that at Pondicherry she received twelve shot wounds, one in her groin and eleven in her legs and that 'on her petitioning His Royal Highness the Duke of Cumberland, he was pleas'd to order her a Pension of £30 a Year'.

and not only obtained a Chelsea pension but, when she died in July 1739, 'her Corpse, according to her Desire, was interr'd amongst the old Pensioners in Chelsea Burying-Ground, and three vollies fired over her Grave'.

The second Chelsea Amazon has an even more curious story. Hannah Snell became something of a celebrity – indeed a sensation – and her life story was published in 1750 by an enterprising bookseller under the title *The Female Soldier, or the Surprising Adventures of Hannah Snell.* In July of the same year *The Gentlemen's Magazine* also published a biography. Consequently the details of Hannah's life – or at least the acceptable details or myth of her life – are readily available, although inconsistent.

She was born in Worcester in 1723 and – in some confusion over a lost love – enlisted in the winter of 1745 in Guize's Regiment of Foot (to become the Warwickshire Regiment) under the name James Gray. She fell foul of a sergeant in her company and was sentenced to be flogged. All was to be disclosed. But no. Although stripped to the waist Hannah was – according to her biography – able to conceal her breasts and her true sex by flinging herself rapidly against the ample gate of Carlisle Castle that had conveniently been chosen as the place of her punishment. Quite how she – bleeding and exhausted – removed herself without revealing her person is a mystery.

Not surprisingly, Hannah was disconcerted by this treatment and when the regiment was in Portsmouth she deserted. But the flogging had not quenched her ardour for the military life and she promptly joined Frazer's Marines. She was sent aboard the man-of-war *Eltham* where her dainty and generally female appearance earned her the nickname 'Molly'. This was the name generally given to effeminate boys or homosexuals

Descriptions of BATTLES by Sea & Land,
in Two Volumes,
From the KINGS Library's at GREENWICH & CHELSEA.

LEFT: *A popular print produced by Dighton in 1801 depicting what were perceived as typical Pensioners of the two Hospitals for veterans of the Army and the Navy: Chelsea on the left and Greenwich on the right.*

in the eighteenth century but – if Hannah's comrades knew her secret – could have been an ironic piece of double bluff. Whatever the facts of the case, the female marine contrived – once again – to earn a good flogging.

This time she concealed her breasts by means of a large scarf that she was allowed to wear around her neck during the ordeal. But Hannah's spirits were not broken. Frazer's Marines were landed at Madras and she took part in the siege of the French colony of Pondicherry, south India. In the process, she got herself wounded in the thigh and both legs. The location of this particular wound was bound to give the game away but Hannah claimed that she crawled from the scene of the fighting and managed to get her wounds treated by an Indian woman.

After four and a half years' military service, Hannah's soldiering days were over and by 1750 she was back in England. She soon realized – or was told – that she had a good story to tell, and to sell, and Hannah was marketed in sensational manner with the floggings – real or invented – adding a lurid sexuality to the tale. Her biography was published and the twenty-seven-year-old Hannah appeared on the stage, dressed in regimentals and marching up and down in, no doubt, a beguiling manner.

The Royal Hospital took her tale seriously. She was admitted to the pension list in 1750 at the standard 5d. per day (raised to 1s. in 1785) to which she was eligible through the wounds she received at Pondicherry. The Duke of Cumberland was alleged to have awarded her an additional £30 per annum, but this seems one of the many myths of the Hannah Snell story.

The truth is grimmer than this pleasing and romantic legend. Hannah's novelty value soon wore off and she failed to sustain popular interest in her stage appearances. She made an unwise marriage, became the landlady of a public house in Wapping, east London, predictably called *The Female Warrior*, became insane and was placed in the Bethlehem Hospital – 'Bedlam' – where she died in 1792. Hannah is said to be buried at the Royal Hospital in an unmarked grave.

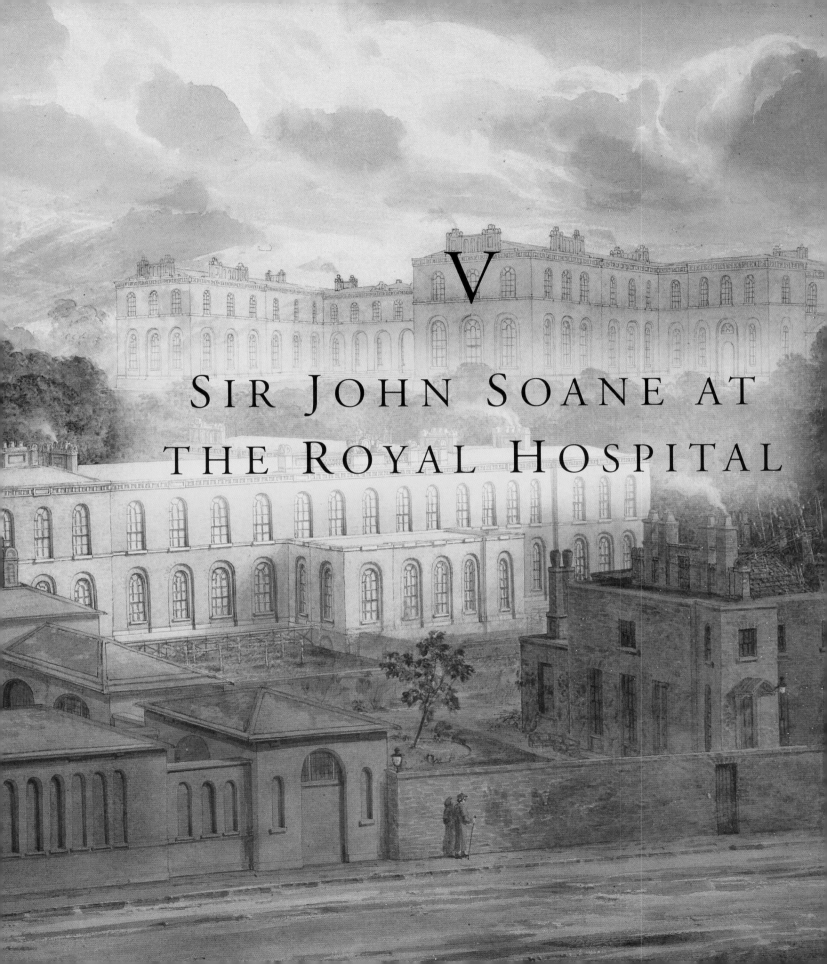

V

SIR JOHN SOANE AT THE ROYAL HOSPITAL

ABOVE: *'Recruiting for the British Army', c. 1770. In the centre a young man takes the 'King's Shilling' as he joins a regiment, while his girl looks on tearfully. The recruiting party consists of an officer, a sergeant, a fifer and a drummer from an infantry regiment.*

PREVIOUS PAGE: *Composite perspective, dated 1818, showing Soane's work then completed at the Royal Hospital. On the left are the Stables and on the right the Clerk of Works House (both viciously attacked in the press in 1815). In the middle is the Infirmary, its south elevation floating in a disembodied manner above the trees. These early buildings were designed in Soane's uncompromising, individual and idiosyncratic classical manner. In the background on the left is the later Secretary's Office, with an exterior designed in deference to Wren's buildings.*

I N MARCH 1807 John Soane secured the post of Clerk of Works to the Royal Hospital Chelsea. This ushered in a twenty-year period of expansion that saw the design and construction of some of the most original architecture ever built in London. The reason for this expansion was simple: the size of the Hospital had to reflect the size of the Army if it was to offer a reasonable number of veterans and invalids accommodation and care. In 1807 the British Army had never been larger. It had to police and defend an empire that straddled the world, garrison Britain against attack and maintain an aggressive war in Europe against Napoleon's French empire. The Regular Army was supported by a formidable volunteer and militia movement with veterans serving in garrisons manning Britain's coastal and inland defences.

Already the veterans of Napoleon's war – with their amputations and mutilations – threatened to overwhelm the space and facilities offered by the Royal Hospital. The alarm had been sounded as far back as August 1794 – after less than two years of war with Revolutionary France – when 1,900 sick and wounded soldiers were landed from transports and sent direct to Chelsea. Twenty-four more beds had to be packed into the existing Infirmary in the south-west wing (with patients moved into former servants' accommodation in the roof space above the Great Hall) and temporary accommodation created in the Hospital grounds. In desperate times Chelsea was not only a refuge for veterans but also for soldiers wounded in battle.

The son of a Berkshire bricklayer, Soane was very much a self-made man and driven by an ambition to succeed that was matched with a genius for his chosen profession. He had been in practice since 1780 – after a few well-spent years in Italy where he honed his natural talents, mingled with other artists and met, among the English Grand Tourists, a number a future clients. Now aged fifty-four, he had an impressive catalogue of works to his credit. He had designed and constructed a bridge and a gaol, as well as church interiors and numerous country houses, and had worked successfully with many powerful and prestigious clients such as the Bank of England and several of its directors.

Even so, Soane was keen to secure the Chelsea job and must have lobbied hard; no doubt some of his numerous clients would have known the Governor, General Sir David Dundas, and put in a good word for him. It was a government appointment and as such carried status and dignity. There was a salary of £220 a year, which was a

ABOVE: *'View of the back part of the Clerk of Works house, as it stood previously to the alterations', a watercolour by a member of Soane's office. These modest and seemingly much-altered buildings, designed originally by Wren, were soon to be demolished for one of Soane's most controversial Royal Hospital buildings.*

Physician and Surgeon

SINCE 1832 THE POSTS OF Physician and Surgeon (P&S) have been combined. Lieutenant-Colonel Wilson Wallace explains that he – and staff of the Infirmary – fulfil a number of distinct medical roles. He operates as the Medical Director to the 350 or so In-Pensioners and the Infirmary operates as a cottage hospital, allowing them to receive care without having to enter the anonymous world of the NHS hospital. The only thing that cannot be done here is major surgery, but Pensioners are brought back to the Infirmary as quickly as possible.

The Infirmary also functions as a nursing home and there are usually forty-five to fifty men being cared for, most of whom will never return to the Long Wards. Even with the most extreme cases – dementia for example – In-Pensioners are cared for within the Royal Hospital. As the P&S points out with pride, 'no one is ever shipped off from here, we deal with all the problems – physical or behavioural – that beset men in old age. We look after them from the "cradle to the grave"'. This means, of course, that the Infirmary has to fulfil a final role – as refuge for the dying. 'In addition the Infirmary has two physiotherapists and offers remedial gymnastics to keep the men fit and on their feet.'

The high quality of care in the Infirmary is very important to the Pensioners. Regularly, in questionnaires they complete, the availability of a high level of medical care comes top of the list. 'It is,' says the P&S, 'very important to them to have "across the board" medical care. If they did not have this, then the Royal Hospital would be like any other old people's home', and this it definitely is not.

considerable sum. In addition the Clerk of Works was entitled to a small house within the Hospital grounds – a perquisite that, as it transpired, Soane was both greatly to enjoy and come bitterly to regret.

On his appointment Soane surveyed the Royal Hospital and concluded that things were in a sorry state. Buildings needed to be repaired and – more to the point – existing facilities enlarged and improved. Most urgent was the Infirmary.

In 1809 Soane was asked to prepare plans for converting the early eighteenth-century Walpole House, standing on the north-west corner of the Hospital site, into a new infirmary. This was a modest solution – and it did not appeal to Soane. He argued that Walpole House was not sound enough or large enough for the purpose. Instead, he

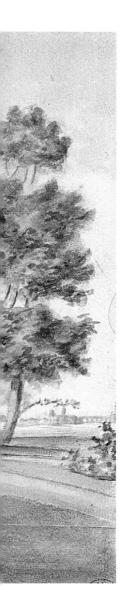

LEFT: *Watercolour of Colonel Gordon's villa, designed in 1810 by Thomas Leverton for the site on which Soane had wanted to build his Infirmary.*

RIGHT: *Staircase hall of Gordon's villa, designed by Leverton in a restrained Neo-classical manner.*

decided that the open land to the south-west of the Hospital, overlooking the Thames, offered an ideal location and he set about designing a massive new infirmary for the riverside site.

A public building on the Thames to rival Wren's earlier Hospital buildings would be a splendid vehicle through which Soane could develop and advertise his own idiosyncratic architectural and constructional theories. But Soane was also making a point about the way in which the Royal Hospital was being managed.

Soon after he had secured the clerkship he discovered that the Crown had agreed to let the site to a Colonel Gordon. It seemed to him that the interests of a public institution were being sacrificed for the benefit of a private individual. To make this point Soane designed his infirmary on a scale that he calculated was needed and to be placed on the only site large enough to receive it – the very one that the Royal Hospital was in the process of letting. In the event Soane was too late. Gordon commissioned the Neo-classical architect Thomas Leverton to design a villa for him which was built by 1810 (and altered in 1825 and 1931, and now used as staff quarters). Having been thwarted in his plan Soane turned his attention to the original brief – the conversion of Walpole House.

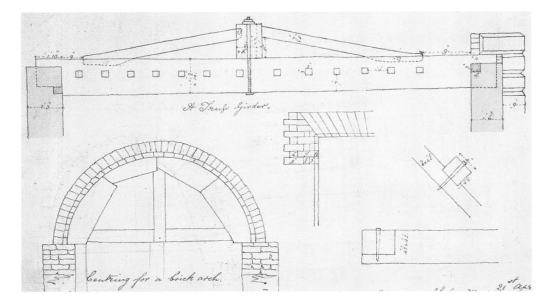

LEFT: *Construction details of the Secretary's Office, designed in 1818, including brick arch, window jamb (in the manner of Wren) and a 'truss girder' with timber elements connected by an iron bolt.*

OPPOSITE: *Detail of the Stables. This bold abstraction and reinvention of the Classical language shocked many of Soane's contemporaries.*

This proved to be a complete rebuild with work starting in mid-1810. Soane was seeking to reinvigorate, almost to reinvent, the Classical tradition – to free it from the unthinking and dead hand of orthodoxy. To do this, he stripped away much conventional ornament and relied on simple forms, on proportion and on almost abstract details to create noble and original – yet still essentially Classical – structures. With its simple brick elevations and arched ground-floor windows, the Infirmary was a good example of Soane's spare and highly inventive manner. Particularly rewarding were the chimney-stacks that were – perhaps curiously – the building's greatest ornament. While Wren

BELOW: *Perspective of Soane's Stables looking north-west through the Chelsea Gate.*

BELOW: *The Stables from the public road, showing corner pavilions and blank arcading to the centre range. On the right is a corner of the front elevation of the Clerk of Works House.*

OPPOSITE: *View of the rear of the Clerk of Works House, painted by a member of Soane's office when building was under construction in c. 1814. Particularly striking are the tall chimney-stacks topped by terra-cotta chimney-pots designed in the manner of gigantic Grecian jars. The house – the subject of harsh criticism in the press in 1815 when it was dismissed as a 'monster' – was demolished in 1858 but two of the Grecian chimney-pots survive in the Museum.*

had given his buildings tall chimney-stacks and placed them to give the long horizontal lines of his ranges much-needed vertical accents, Soane initiated a series of increasingly bizarre designs.

The Infirmary created accommodation for eighty patients as well as a matron and nursing staff, but not the Assistant Surgeon; he was permitted to use the operating theatre and consulting room, when not in use, as a bedroom and sitting room. The completion of the Infirmary not only created space for patients but also freed up other parts of the Hospital for an additional sixty-three In-Pensioners so that the establishment was raised to 539. The building was bomb-damaged in 1941 and subsequently entirely demolished. (In the early 1960s the National Army Museum was built on this site.)

In his dealings with Colonel Gordon – who had pulled down one of Wren's garden pavilions – Soane had claimed that 'to destroy any more of the original buildings must be a matter of very serious regret'. But now it was Soane who swept away a Wren structure: Wren's rambling stable block. The replacement buildings – put up between 1814 and 1817 – were to contain an artificer's court (destroyed in 1941), a new stable and coach house and a greatly enlarged house for the Clerk of Works, who was of course Soane himself.

The Stables – fronting onto the Royal Hospital's West Road – is the most visible and architecturally ambitious of Soane's buildings. Indeed it is one of the most famous of his designs and is now perceived to have marked a key moment in the evolution of his

RIGHT: *Bird's-eye view of c. 1815 showing, in the foreground, part of the stable block, on the left, the Infirmary and, on the right, the Clerk of Works House. Beyond is the now-demolished early Georgian terrace forming Paradise Row.*

BELOW: *Working drawing with measurements from Soane's office showing 'part of the front of the Infirmary'.*

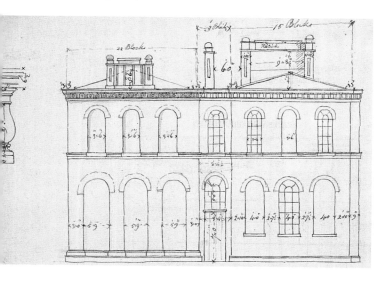

architecture, combining elements of Roman gravity with a reinvention of the language of Classical architecture.

The Stable Courtyard, reached through the central arch, is formed of structures of smaller scale and originally contained stabling and coaches for Hospital dignitaries. The most striking aspects of these lower buildings are their deep-eaved pavilion roofs and elevations that are enlivened by blank arcading – a spirited exercise in the art of 'making small things interesting' that was a characteristic of Vanbrugh's work much admired by Soane.

The Stables possesses a minimalism of form and decoration, and a strange originality that is now found compelling. It was these very characteristics that baffled, outraged – almost frightened – many of Soane's contemporaries. He had been made aware of the effect his radical architecture could have on the popular mind when the recently completed front elevation of his own house in Lincoln's Inn Fields was attacked in the press. The *Morning Post* of 13th October 1812 called it 'a new fangled … ridiculous piece of architecture' and 'a palpable eyesore'. More seriously, he was dragged before the magistrate by the Holborn District Surveyor to answer a charge of having, in the construction of the façade, committed a 'common nuisance'. Soane won the case on a technicality.

In September 1815 an article in a journal called *The Champion* launched a general attack upon current architectural taste in England and on Soane and his works at the Royal Hospital in particular. The new house for the Clerk of Works, wrote the author, was a 'monster in the art of building' while the Infirmary was 'not a jot behind it in absurdity'. Soane was particularly criticized for his 'grovelling pride' and the perverse manner in which he plundered 'from the records of antiquity things in themselves absolutely good but which were never intended in the same place'. His inventive chimney-stacks at Chelsea came in for a rough ride – particular those on the Clerk's house which were topped by gigantic terra-cotta pots in the form of bulbous Grecian jars. The article concluded that, depraved as present taste may be, 'such follies will not pass for wisdom; the public laugh at these extravagances, which are too dull for madness too mad for the soberness of reason'.

The article was written anonymously but Soane thought that he knew the identity of the author. He rushed to Cheltenham to show it to his wife, who confirmed Soane's

ABOVE: *Watercolour from Soane's office of the Gardener's Lodge. This cubical house – a fine example of Soane's original and simple classical manner – does not survive.*

suspicions. The article contained too much inside information to be the work of an outsider. 'Those are George's doings,' declared Mrs Soane of their younger son. 'He has given me my death blow.' True to her word, Mrs Soane was dead within two months.

Soane's turbulent relationship with his son now entered a new and terrible phase. George, frivolous, forever being bailed out of debt by his father, was now held by Soane to be responsible for the death of his wife. Relations were never fully restored and indeed were to take another very nasty turn when, in 1832, Soane discovered that George had had a son by the sister of Agnes, George's wife. The consequence of the alienation of Soane from his children was that the family home in Lincoln's Inn Fields – with its museum and valuable works of art – was left not to a family member but to the nation.

116

ABOVE: *The Guard House under construction in c. 1818. This is an example of Soane's Chelsea style after 1815, when exteriors were designed in deference to Wren's buildings.*

But furious as he was with George, Soane seems to have taken some of the criticisms to heart. Or perhaps it was the Royal Hospital Board whose nerve was rattled, for after 1815 Soane was instructed to design his Chelsea buildings to look 'similar' to Wren's. What is certain is that Soane's later work at Chelsea was designed – externally, at least – in deference to Wren.

The Secretary's Office was commissioned in 1818 for a site on the east side of East Road, flanked by two Wren pavilions – the old Guard House and the old Gardener's Lodge. The Board approved Soane's plan and elevation in February 1818 and ordered the construction to begin immediately on the understanding that 'the Quoins of the Building are to be of stone [as in Wren's buildings] and the cornice similar to the old Guard House'.

Drawings of the Secretary's Office reveal something unusual about the way it was built. The rear (east) walls of the long cross-axial corridors appear to be of cavity construction. If this is the case, here is a pioneering example of what, by the end of the nineteenth century, was to become standard practice. The fact that cavity construction appears to have been used only for the east walls of the corridors suggests that it was part of a system to protect from damp the contents of the cupboards set against these walls.

It was at this period that Soane started to alter the interior of Wren's Chapel. In 1817–18 he changed twelve benches to face the altar (these were reinstated in their original collegiate form in 1920) and in 1834 the original three-decker pulpit was dismantled and divided, and moved from the middle of the Chapel to the east end.

The Surgeon's House – with the more modest Gardener's Lodge that adjoins it (which Soane first extended to create offices and then, after the Surgeon's House was built, to accommodate the Physician) – represents Soane's middle way at Chelsea. Both these

RIGHT: *View of the Secretary's Office of 1818. The exterior, a modest essay in the Wren manner, was based on the design of the two surviving flanking pavilions by Wren.*

buildings on the West Road are essays upon, rather than direct pastiches of, Wren's style and thus stand between the two extremes of the Stable and the Secretary's Office. With the Surgeon's House he included a new Washhouse to increase the bulk of the new building. It is now used by the Quartermaster's Department and as accommodation for the Organist.

At about the time he received a knighthood, in 1831, Soane designed a small structure – a summerhouse for the Chelsea Pensioners – that is one of his last buildings. It was built on land bought in 1826 with a legacy left to the Royal Hospital by Colonel John Drouly, a generous benefactor who had risen from the ranks to become Governor of Cowes. This was the land that had been appropriated by Ranelagh in the 1680s and had been the site of Ranelagh pleasure grounds.

The summerhouse is a strange and fascinating structure – a study in the primitive origins of Classical architecture and a demonstration of the way in which the Classical Orders could have evolved from utilitarian post-and-lintel construction. It is a modest, and often overlooked, masterpiece.

Quartermaster-Sergeant

'ANYTHING THAT MOVES IN THE Royal Hospital is moved by my porters,' announces William Jones with evident pride. A long-serving NCO before coming to Chelsea, Jones now heads a team that is dedicated to the smooth running of the Royal Hospital. 'We do every conceivable thing, mostly to do with the welfare of the In-Pensioners – including looking after their clothing, bedding, furniture in the berths – but also preparing for events such as Founder's Day and the Chelsea Flower Show.'

Like most people who work in the Royal Hospital, Jones and his wife Ann (who was awarded an MBE for her work as a Long Ward Attendant) are smitten by the place – by the buildings, the people and the traditions.

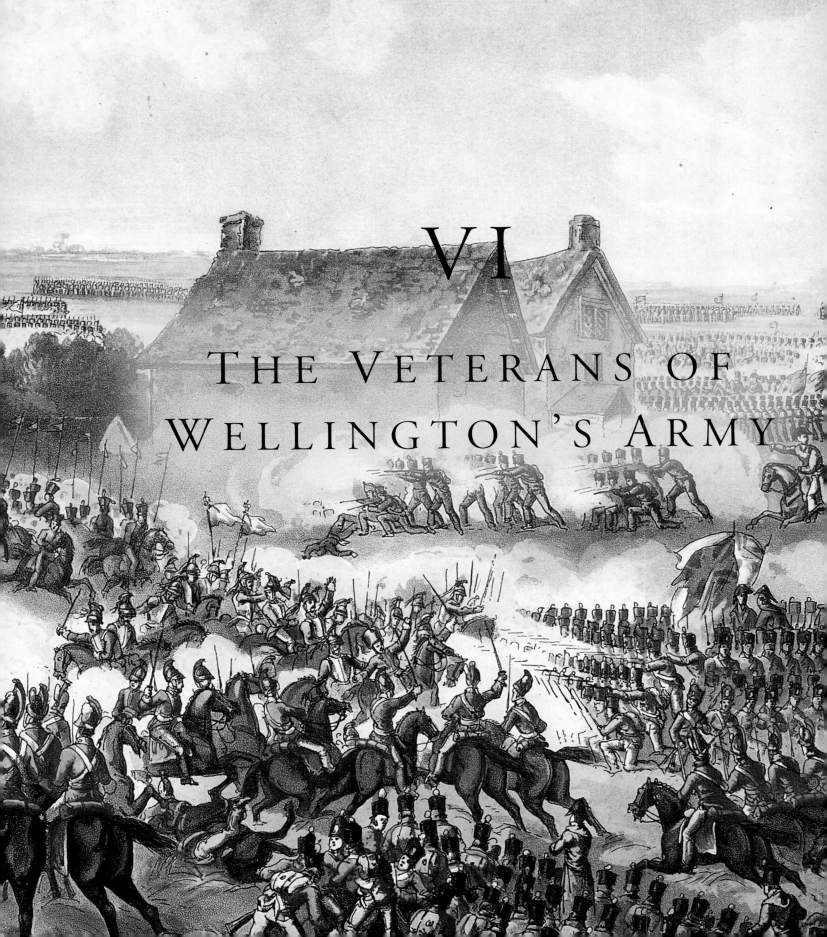

VI
The Veterans of Wellington's Army

ABOVE: *Portrait of the Duke of Wellington by John Simpson. It was presented to the Hospital in 1881 and hangs in the Wellington Hall of the Museum.*

PREVIOUS PAGE: *'Centre of the British Army at La Haye Sainte, June 18th 1815'. The description of this point in the battle had Napoleon and the Imperial Guards in the distance aiming for the centre of the British Army but being defeated by the British square formations 'with great Slaughter'. The farmhouse at the centre of the battle 'was pierced through in every direction with cannon ball; numbers of wounded officers and men crawled in here after the battle, and in the morning it was filled with dead and dying.' Wellington appears on the extreme right of the picture bringing in reserves, 'by which means the last efforts of Napoleon were completely defeated'.*

SOLDIERS WHO HAD taken part in Wellington's campaigns had known Army life at its harshest. But, in late Georgian Britain, much of life was harsh, even for those with money, power and social position. Medicine was primitive – simple operations were agonizing and often fatal – and a callous nature thrived below the Georgian veneer of elegance. For example, slavery was still an accepted aspect of commercial life, with even some of the most enlightened thinkers of the age preferring to see it as a an unfortunate necessity rather than an abomination. The slave trade in the British Empire was made illegal in 1807 but it was not until 1833 that slavery itself was outlawed.

For the poor and powerless life was brutal. The Poor Laws were inadequate and, for those who were forced to steal in order to support life, there were by 1800 over 200 crimes – including trivial types of theft and attacks on property – that carried the death penalty. For even a very minor offence the perpetrator could be confined in the hulks or transported. Without the vote there was no prospect of the common man achieving change through political action. In addition, the harsh sedition laws that had been enacted in the 1790s – in response to a fear of support for the egalitarian principles of the French Revolution – had the effect of crippling, and making illegal, workers' organizations that could have agitated for an improvement in working conditions.

Given these circumstances it is not surprising that a large number of men volunteered to join the Army. Many simply had no choice – faced with starvation or a perilous life of crime, which could end in the gallows or transportation, the Army seemed the least appalling prospect.

This state of affairs was characterized by Wellington, who made a famous and damning observation. Soldiers, he said, were 'taken entirely from the lower order of society' and enlisted for drink. They were 'the scum of the earth'. But the Duke was simplifying a complex issue for dramatic and memorable effect.

During the first decade of the nineteenth century, when the war against France became a stark struggle for national survival, patriotism had stirred the heart and imagination of many a young Briton and those from good, stable and even prosperous backgrounds enlisted. Most of these patriots entered the Regular Army through the

ABOVE: 'Chelsea Pensioners Receiving the London Gazette Extraordinary of Thursday June 22nd, 1815, Announcing the Battle of Waterloo, 1815', detail of a painting by Sir David Wilkie. An oil sketch for the picture is in the collection of the Royal Hospital. The Pensioners and soldiers are shown in front of the Duke of York's public house, Royal Hospital Row. A Light Horseman on the left has arrived with a copy of the Gazette and he relates particulars to his comrades. The paper is in the hands of a Pensioner, a survivor of the Seven Years' War, who was at the Taking of Quebec with General Wolfe. Across the table, having the news recounted to him by an Irish Light Horseman, is a Pensioner who had been at the Siege of Gibralter.

volunteer and militia movement that had rapidly created a huge and colourful citizen army – around 150,000 strong in 1800 – when a French invasion seemed likely.

Typical of this contingent of intelligent and patriotic volunteers was the man who threw a spotlight on the brutal and brutalizing life endured by enlisted men during the Napoleonic wars. John Teesdale's book, published in 1835, is entitled *Military Torture: A Letter addressed to the People of England on the Use of the Cat o' Nine tails in the British Army*. One of the incidents he described had taken place in 1815 when the 28th Regiment was on the field of Waterloo awaiting the arrival of the French Grand Army under Napoleon. On the morning of the battle three of the men were flogged within sight of the advancing army: two had been seen to fall out the evening before to find water and the third had discharged a musket without orders to replace a charge he thought had been damaged by water. Soldiers were expected to fight and die for their country but could not be trusted to do so without the constant threat and example of corporal punishment.

Pensioners who saw tough active service and who lived through a military regime that depended on this barbaric, humiliating and heart-breaking punishment must have found a special peace of mind in the safety and calm of the Royal Hospital – in the dignity of the Great Hall and Chapel and in the quiet of its shady walks. But even these veterans were under a form of military discipline and could be punished.

In 1816 an In-Pensioner – working as an orderly in the new Infirmary – was caught stealing onions from the adjoining vegetable garden. This was deemed 'a crime . . . disgraceful to the character of a good soldier' and would have merited a good flogging in a younger man. But consideration for age was shown and the poor fellow was subjected to a perhaps more cruel punishment. He was ejected from this military Garden of Eden and discharged to out-pension – in effect thrown on to the street with his pension of 5d. or so a day.

Even before its completion and occupation in the early 1690s the Royal Hospital had become part of Britain's military establishment. It was the centre for administration and pensions and it was where military inquiries and courts martial were to be held. It was also a garrison and barrack that could, in times of war or riot, make a major contribution to the defence of London, the Court or the Government.

The active role of the Royal Hospital reached its peak during the French wars. It was the duty of the Pensioners to safeguard the highway between Whitehall and Chelsea

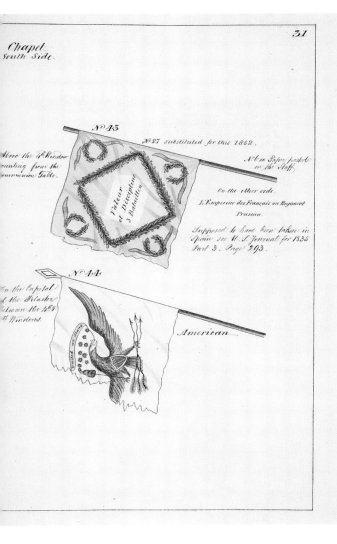

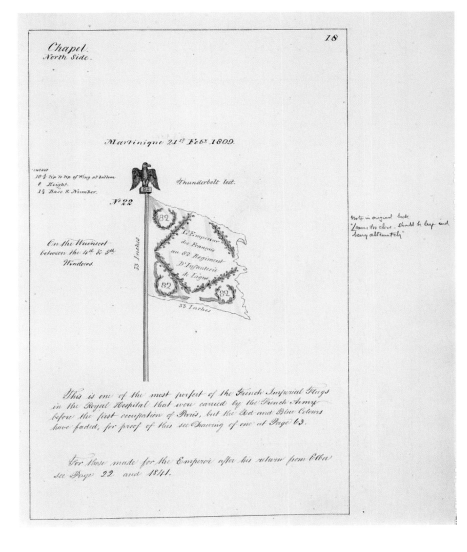

ABOVE: *Drawings from the Victorian manuscript Flag Book recording the captured standards and colours that originally hung in the Chapel: two are Napoleonic and one American.*

and in 1805, Thomas Faulkner wrote, 'Two sergeants, four corporals, and fifty-two privates, who are selected from the most able of the pensioners . . . act as a patrole upon the road from Buckingham-house to Chelsea, for which each man is paid seven shillings and six-pence per month. This patrole was established by royal mandate, on petition of the inhabitants of Chelsea, in the year 1715, the highways at that time being much infested with footpads, and very dangerous to passengers in the evening'.

After the Battle of Waterloo this tradition of service was maintained as part of the state apparatus for keeping the peace and quelling civil unrest rather than repelling foreign invasion. Queen Caroline's trial in 1820 caused such public outrage that riots were feared and the Government took precautions against mob violence. These included fortifying the powder magazine that had been built in the west corner of Burton's Court in 1748 after the Jacobite scare to prevent it falling into the hands of unruly citizens. In addition, the magazine was filled with 3,400 ball cartridges and 300 flints. The force fielded by the Royal Hospital – under the command of the Adjutant – comprised a captain, a sergeant, a corporal and seventy In-Pensioners.

'The Duke of Wellington Showing George IV the Field of Waterloo' painted by Benjamin Robert Haydon.

BATTLE OF WATERLOO

The definitive engagement between Wellington and Napoleon marked a transformation in the reputation of the Army. At the beginning of the nineteenth century it was of far less importance and national pride than the Royal Navy and was supposedly a refuge for desperadoes and drunks: Wellington described common soldiers as 'the scum of the earth'. But, faced with starvation that would in all likelihood end in the gallows or with transportation, many of the poor and powerless had little choice but to join the Colours.

Military life was cruel, involving appalling discomfort and danger, and the threat of arbitrary and unjust punishment. Flogging for quite minor offences – even flogging to death – was to continue into the 1880s. But Wellington's battle plan would have meant nothing if his men had lacked devotion to duty, and had been unwilling or incapable of following his orders. After 1815 the British Army was the most formidable – and respected – land force in the world.

Maurice Shea, the last survivor of Waterloo, died in 1892 and in old age wrote a memoir of the battle:

. . . we withstood many charges of cavalry, the French lancer and cuirassier regiments frequently coming up to the very points of our bayonets and rising around our squares to find an open spot. If they were unsuccessful in this (as they generally were with us) they would retire a distance and make a terrific charge at full gallop. It seemed as though they would ride completely over and through us. They were received with a hail of bullets from the inner ranks of our squares, and when they reached our hedge of bayonets a fearful havoc took place. They were however unable to successfully break our squares once during the engagement; but their loss and ours were terrible. This kind of fighting went on all day from 2 o'clock in the afternoon, when we went into action, until darkness came on.

Shea had enlisted in the 2nd Battalion of the 73rd Regiment of Foot in June 1813. He was joined a month later by Benjamin Bumpstead, a boy of sixteen from Smarden in Kent. On 18th June 1815 they would have faced the enemy together. Standing, kneeling or squatting in a square they peered through the black powder smoke, loading and firing or struggling to present their bayonets. At every moment they expected to be shot, disembowelled by a cannon ball or sabred and trampled by cavalry.

Bumpstead was invalided out of the regiment on 2nd November 1819 at Tricomalee in Ceylon (Sri Lanka). 'To prevent any improper use being made of this Discharge by its falling into other Hands', a description of Bumpstead was attached to his out-pension certificate. He was 'about 22 years of age', 5 feet 7 inches high, with light brown hair, hazel eyes, fresh complexion and 'by trade or occupation a Labourer'. He signed the document with a cross, so he must have been illiterate.

So, four years after Waterloo Bumpstead disappears from the view of history with a pension of 6d. a day. He reappears at Chelsea, where he was admitted as an In-Pensioner on 1st September 1877 and awarded a pension of 1s. 6d. a day. He died on 16th November 1882.

BENJAMIN BUMPSTEAD

'Last survivors of Waterloo in Chelsea Hospital in June 1880'. The veterans are named: John McKay, 42nd Regiment, aged ninety-five, wounded at Badajos and wounded at Waterloo; Robert Norton, 34th Regiment, aged ninety, served in Germany, Holland and France; Naish Hanney, 7th Hussars, aged eighty-eight, served in Peninsula and Waterloo; Benjamin Bumpstead, 73rd Regiment, aged eighty-two, served at Waterloo; Sampson Webb, 3rd Foot Guards, aged eighty-two, served at Waterloo.

LEFT: *Trophies of war on the South Terrace of the Royal Hospital: Dutch cannon dated 1623 and a battery of four French guns captured at the Battle of Waterloo.*

They were armed with obsolete muskets that, when acquired in 1780, were described as 'the old Fusee that was in use during the American War'.

The old muskets were replaced in 1824 and the Hospital's powder magazine was again replenished in 1830. The Pensioners were last employed in an active and direct military capacity in 1848 during the Chartist Riots, when a company of twenty Pensioners helped to guard the British Museum. This military role was maintained until 1854 when the Chelsea Pensioners ceased to be issued with firearms in times of emergency.

During the nineteenth century the Royal Hospital became something of a military Valhalla. Captured weapons and banners were displayed in the Great Hall and Vestibule, captured cannon in its grounds, and monuments to battles, heroes and sombre military events were erected within its loggia and along its walks.

The first record of the Royal Hospital being used to house trophies comes from the first half of the nineteenth century. In 1829 'twelve Standards taken from the Americans, Algerines, Genoese and French during the last war' were presented by George IV for display in the Chapel Royal. In 1835 William IV gave permission for the trophies deposited at St Paul's Cathedral, at East India House and in the Chapel Royal to be transferred to Chelsea. More colours, captured from the Russians, Chinese and Soudanese were deposited in the Royal Hospital during Queen Victoria's reign, but its role as a military shrine reached a climax in 1852 with the funeral of the Commander-in-Chief of the British Army and victor of Waterloo, the Duke of Wellington.

The Chapel and the Great Hall were draped with black cloth and a covered way erected, along Royal Hospital Road, from the London Gate to the vestibule between the Chapel and the Hall. For a week Wellington's body lay in state upon one of the dining tables in the Hall. On 10th November – the first day of mourning – Queen Victoria and the Prince Consort came to pay their respects to the great man. On the following day, when members of the public were admitted, the crowds were immense. Panic overwhelmed the Royal Hospital; the London Gate was locked and several people were crushed to death in the resulting riot and confusion.

The function of the Hospital as a military shrine declined as the nature of the wars fought by the British Army changed from wars of national survival to colonial conflicts. The tradition continues with the lists of battle honours painted on the panelling of the

LEFT: *The body of the Duke of Wellington lying in state in the Great Hall of the Royal Hospital in November 1852, a coloured print after a painting by Louis Haghe.*

BELOW: *Two of the torchères shown in the print now stand in front of the chimneypiece in the Council Chamber.*

Great Hall. Rather picturesquely, above the honours is an array of flags captured during the wars with Revolutionary and Imperial France and its allies in the late eighteenth and early nineteenth centuries, and with the United States during the War of 1812. These flags – replicas of the rotted originals – give the Great Hall a triumphalist air that looks appropriate but that is not authentic; by ancient tradition trophies and achievements of war were hung in churches and chapels to acknowledge the fact that victory in battle was more the work of God than of man. Trophies of arms were hung here for a period of fifteen years from 1890.

Soon after the Royal Hospital opened the standard pension for an eligible old soldier was set at 5d. a day. There were many variations to this: for example in 1774 supplementary grants of around 4d. a day had been made available to severely injured soldiers. In *An Historical Account of the Royal Hospital* of 1805 Thomas Faulkner recorded that there were 20,760 Out-Pensioners each receiving 5d. a day but there were also 650 privates receiving 12d. a day because of 'their great sufferings, and their present distrest situation, having lost their sight in Egypt'. Blind sergeants – of whom there were forty-three – received 18d. a day.

On entry into the Royal Hospital both the standard pension and supplementary grants had to be surrendered. But this did not mean that In-Pensioners had no cash for beer and the like. They were granted 8d. a week each as 'pay' for subsistence, which was in effect pocket money. Faulkner explained that the 'rule-of-thumb' for fixing the level of an In-Pensioner's pocket money was to allow him a sum per week equivalent to his pension per day; the rest was deducted for his accommodation and other standing charges. This rate of weekly pay lasted until 1901, when it was reduced to 7d. and then increased in 1931 to 1s. 9d. In addition, In-Pensioners could earn – and keep – money made by undertaking certain tasks within the Royal Hospital or by virtue of the privileges of their former rank or form of service as, for example, was the case with the senior NCOs described as 'Sixpenny-men'.

The mechanism by which pensions were assessed did not change until 1806. In this year the Secretary of State for War and the Colonies, William Windham, obtained an Act of Parliament that reformed the way in which old soldiers were assessed for pension and for admission to the Hospital. When the Royal Hospital first opened applicants for admission had to have completed a minimum of twenty years' service, or less if invalided out. Now, applicants had to have completed fourteen years' service (only seven if all the years were spent in the East or West Indies) or to have been invalided. The rate of pension was for the first time made dependent on the recipient's rank, service, character and the climate of the places where he had served, as well as his degree of disability. In addition every soldier was given a statutory right to a pension. The result was that the money paid out by the Government virtually doubled.

These reforms were opposed by many of the more conservative members of the military and ruling elite. Indeed Windham's Act was eventually, and seriously, compromised through an amendment that abolished the statutory right to a pension (though the improved rates still applied). The rather crude argument that had been put forward was that in its original form the act rewarded bad soldiers as well as good since it allowed for a soldier discharged for unsatisfactory conduct to be given an early pension for life.

There was also grumbling from In-Pensioners. Those who, under the new rules, received higher than average pensions (due to injury, rank or service abroad) were not awarded higher subsistence money, so in fact they were surrendering more money to the Royal Hospital than their fellows while receiving no extra benefits. Indeed, in some cases, old soldiers eligible for the highest possible pensions would probably have done better as Out-Pensioners.

The amendment to Windham's Act was agreed in 1828, the year in which Lord Palmerston, who had been Windham's successor, left office as Secretary-at-War after nearly twenty years' service. The timing was no coincidence, for Palmerston had proved a reliable supporter of old soldiers and of the Royal Hospital in particular, his greatest achievement being the Army Prize Act of 1811. This piece of legislation ensured that a handsome proportion of unclaimed military prize money was used for the maintenance of the Royal Hospital and its veterans.

Faulkner reported in 1829 that the Out-Pensioners numbered 'upwards of 85,000', an alarmingly high figure – swelled by arduous recruiting over twenty years of continuous warfare – when it is considered that the Royal Hospital, and the system of military pensions of which it was part, was created to support a Standing Army of only 7,000 men. Many of the Out-Pensioners no doubt enjoyed the freedom of civilian life and were aghast at the idea of ending their lives in an institution where the rules of military hierarchy prevailed and freedom was limited. But, as Faulkner implied, there had been one very good reason for trying to become an In-Pensioner.

When the Hospital was established Out-Pensioners were paid their pension annually, and not until a year after they had become eligible to receive it – a thrifty

Adjutant

'THE ADJUTANT IS LIKE THE commanding officer of a regiment,' Brigadier Kim Ross OBE explains. 'I'm responsible for the daily life and welfare of the Pensioners which covers all things affecting their lives other than medical.' The Adjutant is the head of the military hierarchy that gives order and structure to the body of In-Pensioners. 'They are broken down into five companies, each under the "command" of a Captain of Invalids.' To assist the Adjutant are three staff Warrant Officers: 'my right hand man' – the Sergeant-Major, an Assistant-Sergeant Major and the Orderly Room Warrant Officer; these are Royal Hospital ranks and do not necessarily bear any relation to ranks held by the men in the Army.

Brigadier Ross has a deep respect for the old soldiers under his charge. 'They are a remarkable generation, they were brought up with good manners and a natural respect for each other.' The Brigadier is almost humbled by the service and military action many of his charges have seen. Also, as a soldier with thirty-four years' experience, Ross is well aware that active service can produce emotional strains and stresses, and that these can emerge with age.

He recognizes the real benefits that the Royal Hospital holds for the vast majority of In-Pensioners. It literally gives them a new lease of life and he can see why. 'There is an outburst of emotion from the public when it sees the Pensioners in their uniforms. Nothing is too much trouble, they are given very special treatment. And this does wondrous things for them. It shows them that they are respected. They have to live up to the reputation they enjoy. This gives them purpose and pride, keeps them alive.'

OPPOSITE: *Coloured aquatint of Chelsea Pensioners from 'The Costume of Great Britain' by William Henry Pyne, first published by William Miller in 1804. It catalogues the costumes of sixty different types of working men and women.*

accounting ploy to control cash-flow. The consequence of this rule was obvious. Impoverished Pensioners were forced to borrow against their pension and so fell into the hands of loan sharks who would demand a high level of interest on the loan. The result, as often as not, was financial disaster and misery. Faulkner wrote that 'The poor disabled veterans, who enjoyed the pension of Chelsea Hospital, were so iniquitously oppressed by a set of miscreants, who supplied them with money in advance at the most exorbitant rates of usury, that many of them, with their families, were in danger of starving'.

In 1754, in an attempt to reduce the distress into which many cash-strapped Pensioners fell, the Paymaster–General, William Pitt, had obtained an Act of Parliament that allowed the Government to advance a half year's pension half a year before it was due. This clearly made a Pensioner's financial life considerably easier and 'usury was effectually prevented by a clause, enacting, that all contracts should be void, by which any pension might be mortgaged'. Out-Pensioners continued to be paid half yearly until 1815 when an Act of Parliament was obtained that allowed pensions to be paid quarterly in advance and making the life of an Out-Pensioner seem more attractive.

A clothing contract of 1818 shows that the In-Pensioners' uniform had remained virtually unchanged for over a hundred years, although during the reign of George I their hats were furnished with the Hanoverian black cockade – the insignia introduced for all servants of the Crown.

Their uniform could once have produced unfortunate reactions among the public. Soldiers were generally regarded as rough fellows, for none but a fool or a desperate wretch would voluntarily enlist for the brutal life of the Army. Even old soldiers could be viewed in this light. In addition, the Chelsea uniform marked its wearer as the beneficiary of charity (for the Hospital was always partly supported by charity as well as through government funds) and so little better than a pauper.

But, during the Napoleonic Wars, at least, the uniform became a badge of honour. The popular perception of the Chelsea uniform – and of the Pensioner who wore it – is revealed in 1804 by W. H. Pyne. 'The dress worn by these, who are clothed by public bounty, far from appearing a mark of reproach becomes the passport to every good man's esteem ... who can have passed the aged soldier in the uniform of a Chelsea

Published Jan.ʸ 1ˢᵗ 1805, by William Miller, Albemarle Street. Nᵒ 6.

CHELSEA PENSIONERS,

CAVALRY & INFANTRY.

OPPOSITE: *Chelsea Pensioners of the Cavalry and Infantry from 'Costume of the Army of the British Empire' by Charles Hamilton Smith, published between 1812 and 1815. The Pensioners are seen to be wearing the Hanoverian cockade in their hats, tricornes of the earlier rounded form.*

pensioner without having felt a sentiment of respect glowing in his bosom, as a pleasing tribute to the defender of his country.'

In the 1830s significant changes started to be made. At the beginning of the decade senior NCOs (styled 'Captains'), as well as the Adjutant, still wore regular officers' uniform – albeit of an old-fashioned type. No special uniform was prescribed for the Major, who probably wore his old regimentals. By this time officers wore bicorne hats, sometimes decorated with red and white feathers, rather than the more archaic tricornes worn by the men. But in the Royal Warrant of 1833 King William IV granted the Major, Adjutant, the Captains of Invalids and all commissioned officers the privilege of wearing the Windsor Uniform.

This was a pseudo-military uniform that George III had designed in the 1780s for his own use – and the use of his family and some Royal Household staff – while resident at Windsor Castle. It included a long dark blue coat with red facings and collar and brass buttons bearing the star-and-garter emblem, and the motto, of the Order of the Garter whose Knights were installed at St George's Chapel in Windsor Castle. This coat was worn over buff, white or blue waistcoat and blue breeches. No rank badges were worn with this uniform because, despite its military look, it was intended as a civilian costume.

The uniforms of the ordinary Chelsea Pensioners remained unaltered until the 1840s, when a number of changes were initiated and the present-day uniform started to emerge. First, in 1842, breeches and shoes were replaced with dark blue trousers and 'Blucher Boots' and, in 1842, the forage cap, shaped like a shako, was introduced. In 1852 a black stock replaced the old-fashioned white 'roller' stock and in 1859 the late eighteenth-century style of cocked hat, with slightly rounded front, worn on formal occasions was remodelled to form the now-familiar stiff and upright tricorne.

At some point between 1850 and 1860 the colour of the In-Pensioners' coat was changed from red to scarlet, the facing colour made a darker blue, a blue collar added, and the cut altered. This produced a strange hybrid that is part in the manner of the early eighteenth century (long skirts, large pockets with ornamental flaps and deep, turn-up cuffs with buttons), part mid-nineteenth-century military tunic (single row of brass buttons fastened to the neck and topped by a high collar), and part Victorian frock coat.

ABOVE: *Print published in 1823 entitled 'Portraits of Two Chelsea Pensioners. Great Friends!'. They are depicted on their way to the tavern in Jews Row, 'generally singing old military songs on their return'. James Jobson, aged ninety-one, was blind and he is being led by Robert Plumridge, aged eighty-seven. Both men enlisted in the Army in 1741; Jobson entered the Hospital in 1792 and Plumridge in 1802.*

LEFT: *Chelsea Pensioners in one of the Long Wards, a painting of 1879 by Ellen Conolly. A Pensioner reads to a group in front of the berth belonging to James Stevens, formerly of the Grenadier Guards.*

During the 1850s the In-Pensioners' undress uniform – of double-breasted blue frock coat and blue trousers – was introduced, based on the uniform issued in 1846 to Out-Pensioners enrolled in the newly formed Army Reserve but without red cuffs and epaulettes. Also introduced were two types of sleeved, dark blue 'waistcoats' or shell jackets – the double-breasted pattern in 1894 and one with a single row of buttons in 1921 – for informal wear around and within a three-mile radius of the Royal Hospital. This blue undress uniform could be worn with the shako – bearing in red the initials 'RH' – or with a low crowned and peeked 'lounge cap' (or Brodrick cap, introduced in 1868) – popularly called a 'cheese-cutter' – that was emblazoned with a red 'RH' or with the cap badge of the regiment to which the wearer had belonged.

Describing the In-Pensioners' living arrangements in 1829, in the wards now increased in number from the original sixteen, Faulkner wrote:

> they are lodged in 18 wards, to each of which wards two serjeants and two corporals are appointed, with a Matron or Nurse, under the immediate inspection of the

OPPOSITE: *Page of accounts listing the number and rank of In-Pensioners of the Royal Hospital and two companies of Out-Pensioners: one at Windsor and one at Hampton Court. It is stamped 'Royal Hospital Chelsea, Secretary's Office, Feb 20 1874'.*

The present State of the Invalids who are lodged, dieted, and Cloathed within his Ma.ties Royall Hospitall att Chelsea, and which (over and above) receive the weekely Allowance in money hereafter mentioned. —

	per week		In all	per weeke
26: Gentlemen of the Horse Guards, each	00: 3: 6:			4: 11: -
34: Light Horsemen, Each att	00: 2: 0:			3: 8: -
32: Serjeants, Each att	00: 2: 0:			3: 4: -
32: Corporalls Each att	00: 0: 10:		In all	1: 6: 8
16: Drummers Each att	00: 0: 10:			1: 6: 8
336: private Soldiers, Each att	00: 0: 8:			11: 4: -
476:	00: 9: 10:			25: -: 4

Besides their Cloathing Dyett and washing &c.ª

The present State of the Invalides Out Pensioners which are formed into Fowre Companyes.

One Company att Windsor Castle, Consisting of

	per diem	per Annum
1: Captain	0: 4: 0	73: -: -
2: Leiuten.ts each 2.s	0: 4: 0	73: -: -
Ensign	0: 1: 6	27: 7: 6
6: Serj: each, 9.d each	0: 4: 6	82: 2: 6
6: Corporalls 7.d each	0: 3: 6	63: 17: 6
2: Drummers att 7.d each	0: 1: 2	21: 5: 10
150: private Sold.rs att 5.d each	3: 2: 6	1140: 12: 6
	4: 1: 2	1481: 5: 10

Besides Cloathing once in two yeares, which comes to — £ 492: 7: 8:

One Company att Hampton Court Consisting of

	per diem	per Annum
1: Captain	0: 4: 0	73: -: -
1: Leiuten.t	0: 2: 0	36: 10: -
1: Ensign	0: 1: 6	27: 7: 6
3: Serjeants, each 9.d	0: 2: 3	41: 1: 3
4: Corporalls, att 7.d each	0: 2: 4	42: 11: 0
2: Drumm.rs att 7.d each	0: 1: 2	21: 5: 10
80: private Soldiers, att 5.d each	1: 13: 4	608: 6: 8
	2: 6: 7	850: 2: 11

Besides the Cloathing once is two yeares, which is — £ 266: 15: 8:

One Company att Chester of the Same Numb.rs & Pensions	2: 6: 7	850: 2: 11
And the Cloathing once in two yeares is £	- - 266: 15: 8:	

One Company att Tinmouth of the Same Numbers &c.ª	2: 6: 7	850: 2: 11
And the Cloathing once in two yeares is £	- - 266: 15: 8	

Totall for the pay of the 4 Companys	11: 0: 11	4031: 14: 7
Besides Cloathing once in 2 yeares, which is	- - 1292: 14: 8	

Captain of Invalids

THE POST OF CAPTAIN OF INVALIDS was created during the Royal Hospital reforms of the 1830s. Currently there are five Captains, each responsible for a company of In-Pensioners. As Major John Tatham explains, 'The primary duty of the Captains is the welfare and well-being of our Pensioners, so we are directly responsible for them to the Adjutant. Inevitably our responsibilities include monitoring their health, identifying any worries or problems they may have and, as far as possible, helping them live the rest of their lives contentedly'.

Major Tatham, as well as being Senior Captain of Invalids, is the Curator of the Royal Hospital Museum and its Archivist and so, understandably, he has a particularly strong feeling for the style of life and for the buildings. 'We take a great delight in what we have here. The Royal Hospital is a unique establishment, with a great history and tradition and magnificent architecture. All of us feel much pride in being here, in having been invited to undertake these duties.' Clearly, for him, the beauty of the architecture and the dignity of life within the Royal Hospital makes the task of caring for the Pensioners – many infirm – a great privilege. 'One can see the obvious happiness and pride of the old soldiers who live here, men who have served – and often suffered for – their country.'

The Major is full of respect for all the In-Pensioners and, in a quiet way, shows considerable humility when talking about them. 'They are of the generation who have had to endure war and its consequences, an experience that has evaded most of us. They deserve our greatest respect.'

Housekeeper, to take care of the linen and bedding, and to assist in cleaning each ward. Fires are kept in every ward, and the men have all the attendance to render them comfortable.

Gradually the In-Pensioners had ceased dining in the Great Hall. In 1800 one man from each ward was detailed to collect food for his disabled comrades but, increasingly, food was cooked in the wards. In 1805 Faulkner wrote, 'Dinner is served every day (Sunday excepted) at twelve o'clock, and is placed upon the tables for the pensioners, but they never sit down to dine in the hall, as every man is allowed to take his meal to his own berth'. An order of the following year stipulated that the men should take food – part-cooked in the kitchen – to be finished and eaten in the wards, where ranges had replaced the open fires. By 1855 all vegetables and meat were cooked in the wards rather than in the kitchen. The Hall was then used as a recreation room for the In-Pensioners, equipped with billiard tables, and used for the occasional court martial and for entrance examinations for the Army.

The move to oust the In-Pensioners from their Hall seems to have been initiated by the military authorities who wanted to use it for official purposes. The result was that it greatly undermined the sense of community since the Pensioners rarely gathered as a body and their lives became limited by the boundaries of their ward. This state of affairs lasted until 1955, when the Great Hall was once again used as intended – as the convivial and communal heart of the Royal Hospital.

The reforms of Windham and Palmerston pale beside those launched in the 1830s by Lord John Russell. This great Whig politician introduced the first Reform Bill in the House of Commons in March 1831; he became Prime Minister in 1846 for six years and again in October 1865. But from November 1830 until December 1834 Russell was Paymaster-General and Treasurer of Chelsea Hospital.

In this capacity Russell examined the workings of the Royal Hospital with the aim of seeing whether it provided value for money. There was a possibility that this unsentimental reformer would conclude that aged or maimed soldiers could be maintained more efficiently in the nineteenth century than by continuing with a system devised in the seventeenth century. However – and no doubt to the great relief of many – Russell concluded that the Hospital was 'the best machinery for carrying on this branch

RIGHT: *'The Last Muster' by the fashionable Victorian genre painter Hubert von Herkomer. Dated 1875, the picture shows the benches in the Chapel fitted with backs and rearranged by Soane to face the altar. This was turned back to a near-original seating arrangement in 1922.*

of the Public service: insuring at once economy to the National Revenue, due control to the Crown, and justice to the faithful and deserving soldier'. Praise indeed from one of the sharpest – and most progressive – of nineteenth-century politicians.

But, although the Royal Hospital was to survive as an institution, Russell did want significant changes made for he recognized some of those 'abuses which fasten upon all institutions sooner or later'. For example, he observed that, 'the civil offices of the Establishment, instead of being given as the King's Warrants directed to those who had deserved them by *their service or their sufferings* had, in too many instances, been diverted during the last century into mere nominal employments, given without regard to Military service, exercised without reference to the necessary wants of the old Soldiers, and forming only a convenient patronage for the Paymaster of the Forces'.

A Royal Warrant was obtained in August 1833 to carry out reforms in the running and staffing of the Royal Hospital. The poundage deductions on out-pensions were to be reduced from 1s. to 6d. In-Pensioners were to be paid their subsistence allowances weekly rather than quarterly and a wholesale reform of the way in which the Royal Hospital was staffed was set in motion.

Offices deemed unnecessary were gradually abolished and all appointments – except the Clerk of Works – filled by half-pay or retired officers or discharged soldiers. This put the Royal Hospital on an even more military footing. While the post of Captain of Invalids was introduced (and the In-Pensioners organized into six instead of eight companies), offices redolent of ancient, great or royal households, such as Comptroller, Master-Butler, Usher of the Hall, Wardrobe-Keeper and Comptroller of the Coal Yards, were either abolished or replaced by more military and utilitarian sounding appointments such as Storekeeper and Quartermaster. By 1836 these reforms had reduced the salary bill by one-third. If the institution had lost something of its antique charm, it had also gained a future. It had lost many an indolent hanger-on and had greatly gained in efficiency with – in theory – more money being available for the Pensioners and their needs.

Russell also organized the laying out of the south part of old Ranelagh Gardens – acquired six years earlier – as allotments to help keep Pensioners out of 'the gin-shops'. This was the stimulus for Soane to erect his 'Primitive Hut' to serve as a summerhouse and refuge for the Pensioners.

LEFT: *Soane's summerhouse in need of repair. Built in the early 1830s, it is situated in present-day Ranelagh Gardens.*

Other exotic posts were abolished during the late 1830s and 1840s – and more expense saved – including the Inspector of Pensioners at Hanover and the Deputy Treasurer for Prize Business. At this time the clergy attached to the Chapel were reduced from two to one and in 1834 a new man was appointed: the Rev. G. R. Gleig. His appointment shows that Russell practised what he preached – for Gleig was the right man for the job. He had seen active service as a combatant officer before taking Holy Orders and had at first supported Russell's political opponent, the Duke of Wellington – indeed he thought himself close to the Duke.

Gleig was a fascinating fellow. First a soldier, then a cleric, novelist and historian, he wrote three detailed books about the Royal Hospital and ended by becoming Chaplain-General of the Army. Despite his breadth of experience, his keen and informed interest in the Hospital and his genuine concern for its inmates (it was Gleig who added the backs to the Chapel benches for the greater comfort of his antiquated congregation), Gleig's books are not as rewarding as they should be. He was cursed with the maudlin sentimentality of the early Victorian age and contrived to write books that are a mix of fact and fiction with a moral message. Interviews with soldiers become uplifting texts and then adventure stories so that all sense of authenticity is destroyed. Had Gleig been more modest and willing to record old soldiers in their own, unimproved, words, his books would have become vital documents of British oral history. All the same, Gleig's books do contain snippets that throw light on Chelsea life in the 1830s and 1840s.

The *Veterans of Chelsea Hospital* tells, at length, the life history of a number of Chelsea Pensioners, apparently in conversation with Gleig, but all too clearly little or nothing is expressed in the words of the Pensioners themselves. Each story ends with an explanation of why and how the Pensioner found his way into the Royal Hospital. These may well be true.

That of Nele Houett – an Arab Christian or Copt of Egyptian birth who after serving in the British Army had entered the Royal Hospital in the 1830s – is the most interesting because it reveals the sad fate that so often befell old soldiers when forced to live on the small amount of money paid to Out-Pensioners. Houett – or Neal Hewett as he styled himself – enlisted for seven years only but 'offered to enlarge it . . . to work out my claim for a pension'. But before the second period was completed – presumably another seven years to reach the pension threshold of fourteen years' service – Houett's officer suggested that he should make way for a younger man and try for a pension. 'I went with several

BELOW: *Pensioners lighting up, an illustration from* The Illustrated London News. *The gas mantle was situated in the centre of the Great Hall and was removed in 1956.*

others to pass the Chelsea Board. The character which I brought with me might be seen by anyone who will take the trouble to inspect the Chelsea books [and] although not wounded I got the highest pension my period of service would allow – 9d a day.'

So Houett became an Out-Pensioner, 'but 9d. a day, even to a man of frugal temperament, will scarcely suffice to keep the wolf from the door'. So for four years Houett worked as a potboy in a public house near the Royal Hospital – presumably in Jews Row – and then applied 'for admission [to the Royal Hospital] and as my testimonials proved to be in every point of view satisfactory, my application was attended to'.

In *Chelsea Hospital and its Traditions* of 1839 Gleig writes of modest improvements to the life of the In-Pensioners: a 'resource against ennui, as well as a means of restraining them from too frequent recurrence to the public-house, was supplied not many years ago by the erection of a smoking-room – a detached apartment just inside the western gate, furnished with table, benches and a stove'. Here Pensioners would relax with tobacco, cards and dominoes – and, presumably, the occasional glass of liquor.

At the other extreme of convivial relaxation the Hospital had since 1823 been provided with a library – or at least the makings of one – thanks to a donation from a benefactor. This was originally located in the vestry, then from 1829 in the Servants' Hall and from 1964 moved in the former Orangery. With Library and cosy smoking room, and with the gradual disuse of the Great Hall for communal dining, private life in the Royal Hospital was, in the 1830s, starting to assume a decidedly domestic quality that was much in tune with the values of the new, Victorian age.

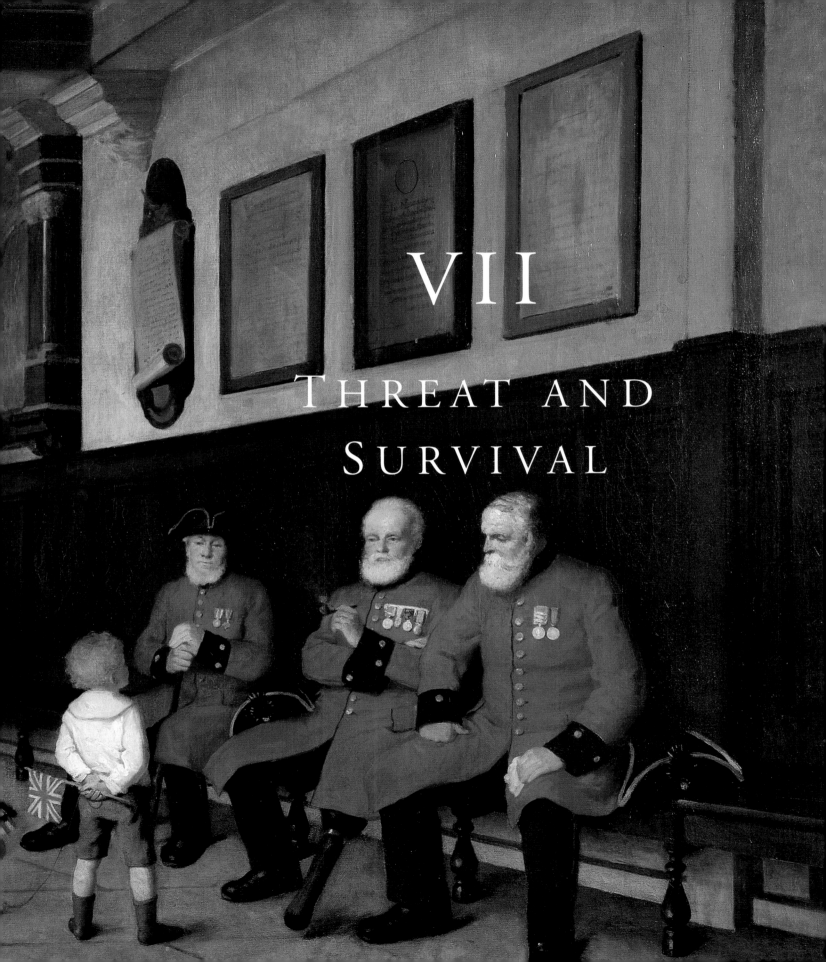

VII

Threat and Survival

ABOVE: *'My Son's Regiment', a painting by Commendator Formilli showing Pensioners outside a shop selling newspapers reading the poster proclaiming the 'Gallant Charge' of the Royal Irish Fusiliers at Talana Hill during the Boer War.*

PREVIOUS PAGE: *'Little Peter and the Chelsea Pensioners', an early twentieth-century patriotic painting by Horace Van Ruith. The Pensioners are assembled in the loggia of Figure Court.*

WHEN LORD JOHN RUSSELL became Prime Minister in 1846 he was succeeded as Paymaster-General by Thomas Macaulay, the writer and statesman. The most important change made in his two years as Treasurer of the Royal Hospital concerned finance. By an act of 1847 the poundage deductions from the out-pensions was discontinued, so that Out-Pensioners now received their pensions in full, and the expenses of the Royal Hospital were met out of Parliamentary Votes. The Hospital also received money due as a result of the Army Prize Act and in the form of legacies and income from rents.

The reforms initiated by Macaulay, and by Russell, did not save the Royal Hospital from a number of attacks on its very existence, however. In 1850 the closing of the Hospital was put forward during an inquiry into Army and ordnance expenditure and was rejected by the Secretary-at-War. But when the Greenwich Hospital for old and infirm sailors closed in 1865–68 the question of Chelsea's future was raised again. The closure of Greenwich – and the expenditure saved – allowed seamen's pensions to rise from 5d. to 9d. a day. So now it appeared that by keeping Chelsea open the minority of In-Pensioners were benefiting at the expense of the majority of Out-Pensioners.

In these circumstances the Prime Minister, William Gladstone, who was intent on reforming the Army, felt obliged to appoint a committee to look into the matter. It discovered that the financial circumstances of the two institutions were very different, particularly with regard to the amount of revenue disposed of by the respective Hospitals (that of Greenwich Hospital being far greater than Chelsea), and concluded that if the Chelsea Hospital were closed an additional 6d. per day could be given to no more than 3,000 Out-Pensioners. The hardship inflicted on the In-Pensioners would be out of all proportion for this meagre gain and the Royal Hospital was saved – but only for the time being.

Largely in response to continuing complaints from Out-Pensioners, Gladstone in 1883 convened another committee to consider the future of Chelsea Hospital. Again, the usefulness of the Hospital was confirmed. It was providing value for money and an admirable service, but various reforms were proposed. The only one acted upon was that staff should be selected from the active, and not the retired, list of officers.

'The Bombardment of Sebastopol'
painted by J. W. Carmichael.

CRIMEAN WAR

The magnificently brave Charge of the Light Brigade against Russian cannon and massed cavalry at Balaclava was quickly seen as an extraordinary example of military dedication, courage and self-sacrifice. The officers and troopers of the five regiments of the Light Brigade understood the suicidal nature of the order but carried it out – and with a will. As Tennyson wrote less than a year after the event: 'Their's not to reason why, their's but to do and die'.

The brigade charged through shot and shell, took the Russian cannon to its front, in a craze of reckless obedience engaged vastly superior bodies of Russian cavalry and then staggered back along Tennyson's 'valley of death' past hovering hordes of dazzled Russian lancers. By the end of the action the once 673-man strong brigade had a mounted strength of only 183 with 247 men killed or seriously wounded, fifty-six left in Russian hands as prisoners, and with 475 splendid horses dead.

The charge of 25th October 1854 almost instantly provided the nation with a compelling image of itself and was seen as a pure and almost painfully glorious yet melancholic manifestation of the British spirit – stoic, brave, dutiful, cheerful in adversity. The Light Brigade – through its heroic act of obedient self-sacrifice – reinvigorated the nation.

Men who were actually present – even instrumental – in this epoch-making event, and who survived, soon seemed more myth than blood-and-flesh reality. Such a legend – who once walked the wards of Chelsea Hospital – was Trooper Sheridan. The man who rode in 'The Charge'.

In October 1875 – twenty-one years after the charge – Sheridan was present at the first Balaclava Banquet, a commemoration held at Alexandra Palace in north London. He was one of several Balaclava veterans from Chelsea Hospital to attend. The others were Jacob Hanson and Thomas Wroots of the 11th Hussars, and Dennis Connor and Robert Grant of the 4th Light Dragoons (later renamed the 4th Hussars).

During the banquet Sheridan, and a number of his fellow veterans, spoke of the charge and their accounts were published in *The Illustrated London News*. Sheridan said,

> I belonged to E troop of the 8th Hussars, under Colonel Shewell and Captain Lascelles . . . We were under Lord Cardigan and a pluckier soldier never drew a sword . . . On the morning of that memorable day we stood with our horses saddled ready for any emergency. Lord Raglan and his staff were on the hills above us, surveying the Russians with their field glasses . . . Presently Captain Nolan . . . came

up with a paper from Lord Raglan, and we imagined at once that we were to move. The order was . . . to charge the guns left by the Turks [now in Russian hands] in order, I suppose, that we might recover them from the enemy. Captain Nolan's words were . . . 'My Lord, charge on those guns'.

I know when I heard the order given at first I said, 'God forgive me! But every man must do his duty'. Well, we merely trotted at first, but when we came within cannon-shot we put our horses into a canter. Captain Nolan, unfortunately, was killed before we got to the redoubt. The Russians met us with a heavy cannonade. They had fired the five guns left by the Turks, so that when we got to the redoubt we found that it was empty, for the Russians had limbered up the guns and taken them . . .

My opinion is that when we found the guns had been removed we ought to have stopped, but poor Nolan was not there to explain matters, and somehow or other, the devil being in us, I suppose, for fighting . . . we went full gallop at the enemy. It was almost dark, with smoke and fog, and you did not know where you were until you ran against a Cossack. You know your blood soon gets warm when you are fighting, and it didn't take us long to find out that that we had nothing to do but to give them a point as good as their cut. I got a cut with a sword on the forehead at the guns. It was not much, but it has left this scar. I remember it now. It was frightful.

It was with these memories that Sheridan entered the Hospital in 1874. He died in 1878.

TROOPER SHERIDAN

Anthony Sheridan was born in 1817 at Carnew in County Wicklow, Ireland, and on 18th August 1836 travelled to Dublin where he enlisted in the crack cavalry regiment, the 8th Hussars. He served with the regiment for twenty-four years and was discharged at Canterbury in November 1860 at the age of forty-three, having completed the period of his enlistment. His character and conduct is recorded as having been 'good' and it was noted that he was 'in possession of the Crimea and Turkish medals and four clasps e.g. for [the battles of] Alma, Balaklava, Inkerman and [the siege of] Sebastopol and . . . two good conduct badges'.

Sheridan remained a private during his entire service, perhaps because he was court-martialled in 1839, 1845 and 1847, twice for being absent without leave. In all cases he was sentenced by his commanding officer to short periods of imprisonment with reduction in pay.

The Colonel of the 8th Hussars at the time of Sheridan's discharge was Lieutenant-General the Earl of Lucan – the man who commanded the cavalry division at Balaclava and who passed the order to Lord Cardigan, the commander of the Light Brigade, to charge the Russian guns.

The Balaclava Banquet, held at Alexandra Palace in October 1875 for survivors of the battle twenty-one years earlier.

ABOVE: *Early nineteenth-century watercolour of the Orangery built by Vanbrugh for Sir Robert Walpole. The long, south-facing arm of the building was converted into the Hospital Library (above right) in 1964.*

RIGHT: *The short arm of Vanbrugh's Orangery became the Roman Catholic Chapel of St Michael in 1963.*

RIGHT: *A Long Ward in c. 1920. The Pensioners are sitting close to the range or looking out of the windows, through which sunlight floods in.*

The construction of a Roman Catholic chapel was suggested as nearly a fifth of the In-Pensioners were Catholics, but in the event only a Chaplain was appointed.

The agony was to continue. In 1894 the Secretary of State for War convened yet another inquiry to consider the Hospital's abolition. The Commander-in-Chief of the Army, the Duke of Cambridge, made it clear that in his opinion the Royal Hospital was serving a worthwhile purpose because it was saving old soldiers from dying in the workhouse. The committee concluded very wisely that the Duke's view was their own.

And so the Royal Hospital entered the twentieth century, somewhat enlarged, reorganized, reformed – and closely examined and tested – and largely fulfilling the job for which it had been founded over 200 years before. Wren's plan was flexible enough to permit whatever physical changes had proved necessary. More to the point, there was still adequate demand in 1900 for the 530 or so berths that the Hospital offered, a demand

The next attack on the Royal Hospital was direct – and physical – in its nature. The First World War pioneered many horrors in warfare, including aerial attack deep into the enemy's heartland with unsuspecting non-combatants among the victims. On the night of 16th February 1918 the Royal Hospital experienced this new variation on the art of war. German bombers, flying high to avoid anti-aircraft fire and almost blind, followed the sparkling course of the moonlit Thames in their attempt to identify and destroy targets. So, large and distinctive riverside buildings such as the Royal Hospital were particularly vulnerable, especially if they were also legitimate military targets as

that was not affected in any significant way by the introduction of the Old Age Pension in 1908.

the Hospital, arguably, was. The eastern end of the north-east wing of Light Horse Court was obliterated by a massive 500-pound bomb. The victims were not active military personnel, or even old soldiers, but the wife, two children and niece of a Captain of Invalids, who also died in the attack.

After the war the wing was reconstructed in replica but with a modern and replanned interior. During the 1920s the Hospital was modernized in many minor but significant ways with the aim of making it more comfortable for the Pensioners and functional. New bathrooms were put in to enable all the men to have a weekly bath. Lifts were installed in the east and west wings in 1925 and 1931 and central heating in the wards in 1930–31. At the same time a wireless set, with headphones in every berth, was provided, as were reading lights.

RIGHT: *Solemn-faced Pensioners reading and hearing the news from the Front in 1916, during the First World War. At this date the Pensioners ate in their wards rather than in the Great Hall, where they are gathered in this photograph.*

LEFT: *Berth belonging to In-Pensioner J. Bines photographed in 1950. A spring mattress has now replaced the original plank bed. A picture of Winston Churchill figures prominently among the personal possessions that he brought with him to the Hospital.*

RIGHT: *A Pensioner moving his bedding from the east wing after a bomb had hit the north-west corner of Light Horse Court in October 1940.*

When war seemed imminent in 1938 the Royal Hospital was determined not to be caught unprepared, and trenches to serve as air-raid shelters were dug in the lawn immediately to the north of the Chapel and Hall and also in Infirmary and Light Horse Courts. In addition, shelters were created in the undercroft below the Hall and Chapel and in a tunnel below the south end of the west range. When war broke out about fifty Pensioners and some staff were evacuated to Rudhall, near Ross-on-Wye, and art treasures were removed for safe keeping to Montacute House in Somerset. Most of the Pensioners and staff, however, stayed at Chelsea, sleeping in the shelters and in the ground-floor berths and in ground-floor corridors.

The first attack came on 28th August 1940. Now veterans of many a petty colonial engagement, of the rumbling conflict on the North West Frontier, of the ill-starred Boer War – and of the carnage of the First World War – were once more in the firing line, the target of enemy action. Two bombs fell and exploded in Burton's Court but no one was killed or injured. In September a bomb exploded opposite the Stable, forming a crater in West Road, and smashed the gas and water mains and the public sewer. Again, there were no casualties. The following month, on 16th October, three bombs fell near the Infirmary, which was still in use, and the patients were evacuated. Luckily, two of the bombs failed to explode and no one was injured.

ABOVE: *Pensioners taking shelter in the crypt of the Chapel in 1940.*

Three attacks in less than three months was not just bad luck. The relative proximity of the Royal Hospital to important military targets such as the Thames bridges, the road along the Chelsea Embankment and the Battersea and Lots Road power stations made it particularly vulnerable. Indeed, as in the First War, it was itself a legitimate target, given its quasi-military function and was certainly easy to identify from the air. In late October, just as patients were returning to the patched-up Infirmary, a stick of four bombs straddled the Royal Hospital. Three exploded in the courts and garden but one – the third in the stick – destroyed the main staircase in the east range.

All was quiet for a few months, but the worst was far from over. On 8th March 1941 a cluster of about sixty incendiary bombs fell across the Hospital grounds. Six fires started in various parts of the buildings, but all were extinguished by the staff and old soldiers without the assistance of the Fire Brigade. On the same day five high-explosive bombs fell near Buckingham Palace, destroying the North Lodge, and the Café de Paris near Piccadilly Circus was also hit, killing thirty-four people and injuring eighty.

Just over a month later, on 16th April and during one of the heaviest London air raids of the war, disaster finally struck. A monstrous weapon – a massive naval mine filled with 1,620 pounds of hexamite explosive and dropped by parachute – hit and destroyed the east wing of Soane's Infirmary. Now the first casualties were inflicted.

ABOVE: *General the Hon. Sir Neville Lyttelton PC GCB, Governor of the Royal Hospital from 1912 to 1931, in Soane's Infirmary. He clasps the hand of In-Pensioner W. Piner, a veteran of the Crimean War.*

ABOVE: *Wynford Vaughan Thomas of the BBC, with Colour Sergeant J. J. Jones, talking to a nurse outside Soane's Infirmary, which was devastated by a bomb on 16th April 1941.*

ABOVE: *In-Pensioner Samuel Pope, killed at the Hospital by enemy action in 1941 aged 100.*

OPPOSITE, TOP: *Drawing by Norma Bull inscribed 'Rocket Incident, Chelsea Royal Hospital. Civil Defence Services in Action'. It is dated 3rd January 1945, the day the north-east wing was destroyed.*

OPPOSITE, LEFT: *The destroyed north-east wing.*

OPPOSITE, RIGHT: *The wing reconstructed, externally as a replica of Wren's original building.*

Four nurses, the wardmaster and eight Pensioners were killed outright. Later the same night another mine fell in Franklin's Row and a bomb opposite the Infirmary, together causing further damage to the Royal Hospital. During the same night Wren's St Mildred, Bread Street, was levelled, leaving only the tower standing, and a bomb crashed through the north transept of St Paul's Cathedral and smashed into the crypt. St Paul's was – of course – repaired, but so low was the value placed on historic buildings in the aftermath of the Blitz that the substantial remains of Soane's Infirmary were eventually demolished – a very sad and unnecessary act.

But the devastation of the Infirmary did not mark the end of war-time attacks on the Royal Hospital. In the late summer and autumn of 1944 the blast of V1 flying bombs exploding around Chelsea damaged the Royal Hospital and, on 3rd January 1945, a much more powerful V2 rocket landed on the north-east wing of the Hospital – the very wing that had been rebuilt after bomb damage inflicted in 1918. In this attack five residents were killed including an In-Pensioner who was standing in the Chapel when the rocket exploded. Nineteen people in and around the Hospital were wounded.

The Royal Hospital had survived once again, though with some damage. Among the other survivors were the soldiers who in the second half of the twentieth century opted for in-pension. William Avery – a former quartermaster in the Royal Army Medical Corps – described in a letter addressed 'to whom it may concern' the domestic amenities of the establishment in 1951, when he first entered the Hospital:

"Rocket Incident, Chelsea Royal Hospital."
Civil Defence Services in Action. 3.1.45.

Messing was then a very crude affair. There was no Dining Hall or Central Messing, food being brought from the Kitchen to the Long Wards where it was divided. The food was well cooked and very palatable when it left the Kitchen but entirely lost any appetizing appeal by the way it was served out. It arrived at the Long Wards in the large circular galvanized iron dishes, dixies and tea cans from which it was divided with large ladles and very long spoons into plates or basins. Tea was made in the Long Wards by boiling a black iron kettle on the coal fire and was mashed in a teabucket.

There was no Infirmary and the Roman Catholic Chapel had not yet been built. As to the living quarters, the only furniture in the berths was a small chair; wooden settles and forms around the fire provided the little comfort and place for socializing that the Pensioners were able to enjoy. In fact, 'things were so discomforting that I obtained permission to revert to out-pension'.

When, in 1969, Avery applied to return to in-pension, he was asked by the Governor whether he noticed any changes. In the gloom of the post-war years, before the buildings had been repaired and refurbished, the Hospital had seemed to Avery like a prison. But in the intervening years the north-east wing had been rebuilt, replicating Wren's original building for officers although internally altered to create additional Long Wards, an Infirmary had been built in a new position on the east side of the Hospital, overlooking Chelsea Bridge Road, and Vanbrugh's Orangery had been restored and replaced with a new Library and the Roman Catholic Chapel. The dining arrangements had been reformed and the comfort of the Pensioners had become a priority. To the Governor's question, Avery replied, 'Now it is a Home'.

The last of the Pensioners to have fought in the First World War died in January 2002. Albert Alexandre joined the Guernsey Light Infantry in September 1917 and after seven weeks' basic training arrived in France. The regiment had just suffered a frightful mauling during the advance at Cambrai when it lost nearly 700 men in ten days, but despite this morale remained surprisingly high. Christmas celebrations gave rise, as the regimental history records, to 'an unbounded vein of hilarious humour and uproarious chorus of celebration of a Christmas that many knew would be their last'. Then came news that the regiment was to be posted to the most dreaded of locations – the Passchendaele-Ypres sector – an area of flooded trenches and

continuous fighting that quite literally stank with the carnage of nearly three years of bloody fighting.

Alexandre arrived at Passchendaele on 18th January 1918, aged sixteen and three months. The place was indeed hell – the front consisting of little more than waterlogged shell holes with gas shells, mortars, snipers' rounds and barrages a daily ordeal. 'I expected it to be bad', said Alexandre, 'but it was a lot worse than I expected. Mud, snow, ice, everything'.

Then in March came the long-dreaded German offensive. Despite the preparations that had been made, the German attack – led by specially trained and equipped shock troops – was spectacularly successful in its early phases. The British Army seemed to crumple. After years of stalemate, with the front moving little more than yards in either direction, the Germans now swept west. Within days they had advanced ten miles in Alexandre's sector and the Guernsey Light Infantry were dangerously outflanked at Passchendaele. The regiment withdrew, was ordered to make a stand to hold the line, came under heavy attack and then had to retreat again when the battalion on its right was overrun. The retreat was chaotic and bloody. But incredibly, the British Army pulled itself together and a line was held. Ultimately, it was the German Army that suffered most during this attack. The early gains had been spectacular but it had failed to break the British. This was fatal. The Germans had gambled their last resources – material and morale – on this attack. It had not won the Germans the war – indeed it had lost it for them. The Allied armies remained on the field and – with the arrival of US forces – were daily growing in strength while the German Army had used its last reserves and not achieved a decisive result. It was now just a matter of time before Germany collapsed.

Alexandre had survived seven months of fighting, fighting as tough and frightening as any during the war. What had it been like? Alexandre is cautious. 'I wouldn't like to

Parnell's judgment of his former Afrika Korps opponents is generous. 'They were bloody good soldiers, very efficient. The fighting was clean. To me it was a war of machines – machines not men were our targets. We didn't fire at Germans to bring them down when they ran from their vehicles, and they didn't fire at us.'

BATTLE OF EL-ALAMEIN

'It was just hell for ten days – chaos – a complete cock-up.' This is the pithy comment of Tom Parnell who fought at El-Alamein. The battle that Tom Parnell experienced as loosely controlled military chaos is now known to history as the first significant British land victory of the Second World War. Fought in North Africa from 23rd October into early November 1942, and choreographed by General Montgomery, it was the British counter-thrust that stopped the combined German and Italian forces in their victorious drive through Egypt towards Alexandria.

The 10th Hussars, which Parnell had joined as a tank commander, were in the 2nd Armoured Brigade of the 1st Armoured Division that was part of X Corps. This brigade had ninety-two Sherman tanks – recently issued and, in 1942, state-of-the-art with their powerful seventeen-pounder guns. This force gave the 2nd Armoured Brigade a massive punch. The X Corps, commanded by General Lumsden, also contained the 10th Armoured Division. The task of X Corps was to pass through two corridors in the deep Axis minefields that would be created by the Royal Engineers and infantry of XXX Corps. The 10th Hussars and the rest of the 1st Armoured Division were to pass along the north corridor – codenamed Star. Once through the corridor the tanks were to advance and fan out behind the outflanked enemy positions to seek and destroy the enemy's tanks. This, anyway, was Montgomery's plan.

At first light on 24th October the 10th Hussars moved forward as planned, immediately behind the 5th Black Watch.

But, as dawn broke, the X Corps had still not got out of the minefields and, as visibility improved over the battlefield, the 10th Hussars discovered that this was a very dangerous place in which to be stuck. As Parnell remembers, all was now 'utter chaos. We had hit a minefield that had not been known about so no route through it had been cleared. Engineers got to work but this led to a twenty-four-hour delay in our attack on our objective, Kidney Ridge.' While the crews of hundreds of stalled and closely packed vehicles started to contemplate their frightening predicament the Axis response started. 'Between ten and eleven in the morning,' Parnell recalls, 'the Germans started to throw heavy stuff in – it was bad.'

As well as the unexpected minefield there was a third that had not been known about so was uncleared. There were also concealed enemy strong points and these were halting the move forward. The corridor through the enemy minefield in which Parnell and his Sherman were sitting was only about 8 yards wide. Vehicles could not pass each other nor could vehicles turn to retreat or manoeuvre to hide from the enemy gun-spotters who would get to work with a will as the sun illuminated the British column. They were all – potentially – sitting ducks.

There were three choices facing the commanders of X Corps as its advance ground to a halt in the early hours of the morning. To advance into the unknown darkness and risk being blown up by mines or hit by well-concealed enemy anti-tank guns. To stay where they were and to present the enemy

gunners with a perfect – unmoving – target. Or to disperse into the ground on either side of the corridor, with the risk of being blown up by mines. All things considered, there was really only one decision that could be reached and the vehicles were deployed into the unswept ground. The 10th Hussars were deployed without losses. Immediate catastrophe had been avoided but the situation remained grim.

For Parnell the early stage of the battle was punctuated by a series of stark memories. But, in the way of

TOM PARNELL

Tom Parnell was born in Bolton, Lancashire, in 1918 and in 1935 enlisted in the Territorial Army, joining the Duke of Lancaster's Own Yeomanry. At the outbreak of war he was with the Royal Dragoons and in 1941 found himself serving with the 10th Hussars. He was discharged from the Army as a Squadron Sergeant-Major in 1958 and entered the Royal Hospital in 1986.

British soldiers, the horror was made palatable through the application of a heavy dash of gallows humour. 'After our first night of action we pulled out to refuel. We were shelled and one dropped close by a man called Ledger. He was a tough cockney, intelligent and an atheist. He could talk the padre into knots over religion. But when Ledger was hit,' smiles Parnell, still relishing the irony of the moment, 'he said the Lord's Prayer aloud and asked for his mother'. What happened to him? 'Oh, he died a few minutes later.'

By midday on the 25th Montgomery, while accepting that his original battle plan had been compromised by the delay in the minefield, resolved to press on with the main element of his plan – to launch his major attack in the north in an attempt to penetrate the Axis front a few miles south of the coast and capture the coast road.

Although wrong-footed, the German troops counter-attacked with characteristic aggression and determination. Shortly before sundown the British armour in front of Kidney Ridge was attacked by the 15th Panzer Division, whose tanks rolled in with the sun behind them. The battle was brutal, but at last light the panzers pulled back. The British tanks had gained a small – but significant – triumph. The next day fighting continued all along the front and was particularly severe around Kidney Ridge where a salient was driven into the enemy's positions.

Although the main British thrust was maintained in the north, things were going painfully slowly. Tension in London reached breaking point with a furious Churchill asking, 'Is it really impossible to find a general who can win a battle?'

On the 27th Rommel struck back with the main target being the British 1st Armoured Division. But, by the end of the day the Axis forces had received a very bloody nose indeed.

Parnell lost a tank during the action. It was hit, in the front of its body, by an 88 armour-piercing round. A fire-ball engulfed the interior of the tank but the crew escaped – except the driver. His hatch, damaged by the hit and with the gun barrel in the immobile turret wedged above it, would not open enough to allow escape. Also, because the tracks of the tank had sunk into the soft sand, the driver could not open the escape hatch in the base of the tank. Stanley Tate had to be left to die, trapped in the burning Sherman. There could be few worse moments in war, to have to stand by helplessly and watch a comrade die in such horrendous circumstances.

Parnell acquired another tank – but this too was hit and Parnell wounded. He had his head out of the top of his tank when an armour-piercing round hit the armour a few feet ahead of him. For Parnell, with lacerated throat and temporarily blinded, the Battle of El-Alamein was over.

ABOVE: *In-Pensioner Alf Amphlett BEM, a veteran of the Second World War and holder of the British Empire Medal and the Polar Medal.*

say if I killed a German – that's something that I never said to anyone. I don't like to think about it. All I can say is that it was hand-to-hand fighting and you had to defend yourself.' After the fighting was over Alexandre caught what was called 'Trench Fever', spent some time in hospital but had returned to his regiment by 11th November when news of the Armistice came through. 'We jumped for joy but some of us couldn't believe it' – not until they marched past German troops who were packing up their belongings as they prepared to march home.

With the war over Alexandre was quickly demobilized. But what was he to do? Having reflected on his future he resolved to rejoin the Army – this time opting for the Royal Artillery. By 1940 Alexandre had served twenty-two years with the Colours, had married, and was considering retirement. Then came the emergencies of the early years of the Second World War and he remained in the Army – training recruits in Britain and India – until the war ended.

In March 1994 Alexandre went to the Royal Hospital for a three-day trial. He was apprehensive but stayed and found peace and contentment. By the time he was interviewed by Philip Ziegler for his book *Soldiers* Alexandre was blind and deaf but, observed Ziegler, he was a 'man of radiant contentment' even though he was living with the memory of the comrades of his youth – the men who had died at Passchendaele nearly ninety years earlier.

In-Pensioner Alf Amphlett survived to recount his memories of the Second World War. He joined the Worcestershire Regiment in 1937, was transferred to the Royal Artillery and – due to his pre-war experience as a technician in foundry work – had been transferred to the Royal Army Service Corps by the time it landed in Normandy on D-Day +7 in June 1944. Amphlett remembers those early days of the invasion as 'all dust and flies, flies breeding on the dead cows and dust killing the trees'. Despite landing 'with a tool box and spanners rather than a gun', Amphlett was attached to 1st Commando Brigade and with them crossed the Rhine and was in Denmark when the German Army surrendered.

Amphlett stayed in the Army after the war and reached the rank of warrant officer. In February 1956 he was 'the only REME chap with a party of fifty Royal Engineers' who were sent to the Montebello Islands for the nuclear bomb tests. For his services – as base engineer maintaining a variety of vehicles and plant (which was a 'miracle' of enterprise according to a contemporary official report) – he was awarded the British Empire Medal. In November 1956 Amphlett joined the Royal Geographical Society's Antarctic Expedition led by Vivian Fuchs. He remained in the Antarctic – as base engineer in a party of twenty-one men – for two and a half years. For this he was awarded the Polar Medal.

In-Pensioner Robert Middleton has an extraordinary war record. He was taken prisoner twice: by the Germans at Oudenarde in 1940, while serving with the 2nd Batallion The Buffs, and in Korea in 1951. The first time, he escaped as the prisoners were being moved to avoid the Russian advance and joined the US forces; the second time he was with the Gloucestershire Regiment and was the last man on the truck leaving the camp at Choksong when the prisoners were released. He is, not surprisingly, the holder of the Military Medal, awarded in 1953.

In-Pensioner Myles Foster was a corporal in the 3-inch Mortar Platoon of the Royal Leicestershire Regiment at the beginning of the Korean War. In November 1951 his battalion was in action on Hill 355, defending it against the Chinese who had entered the war on the side of the communist North Koreans. In June a year later Foster was wounded when his team was sent to act as a Forward Observation Post for the Mortar Platoon and evacuated to a Canadian field hospital. He returned to England by troopship and air and well remembers, shortly after arriving in Leicester, the regiment marching through the city with Colours flying. Foster joined the Royal Hospital in 1997.

LEFT: *Pensioners seated in the loggia of Figure Court, a photograph of 1920. Wren designed the loggia so that, when the sun is low in the sky, light reaches the benches at the back.*

NELL GWYNNE

RIGHT: *Portrait of Nell Gwynne by Simon Verelst.*

BELOW: *'King Charles II and Nell Gwynne at Chelsea Hospital', a mid-nineteenth-century painting by Edward Matthew Ward.*

THE INSPIRATION FOR THE FOUNDATION OF the Royal Hospital came from Nell Gwynne, goes the legend. The favourite among Charles II's many mistresses, Nell was touched by the plight of the old soldiers and persuaded the King that something must be done for them. So the Hospital was established not so much to deal with a social problem or to house an armed bodyguard of veteran soldiers for the King – and at the same time liberate his new

LEFT: *Portrait of Louise de Keroualle, Duchess of Portsmouth, from the studio of Sir Peter Lely.*

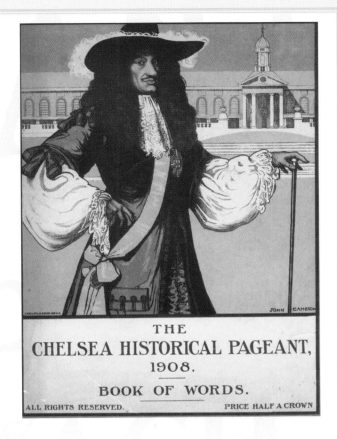

RIGHT: *Cover of the programme for a pageant celebrating the history of Chelsea.*

THE
CHELSEA HISTORICAL PAGEANT,
1908.
—
BOOK OF WORDS.
ALL RIGHTS RESERVED. PRICE HALF A CROWN

Standing Army from responsibility for the men who were no longer fit to serve – but to acquiesce to the wishes of his kind-hearted mistress.

From the middle of the eighteenth century the legend acquired sentimental and popular appeal. Nell came from a poor family and was first heard of selling oranges at the Theatre Royal, Drury Lane, before making a name for herself as an actress. Her background was different from that of some of her better-born rivals such as Louise de Keroualle. She was passed from the protection of one admirer to another – from the actor Charles Hart to Charles Sackville, Lord Buckhurst, and to the King, whom she called her 'Charles the Third'. As he lay dying Charles famously demanded of his brother, James II, 'not to let poor Nelly starve'.

The story of Nell Gwynne was published and became widely known; a tavern close to the Hospital was named after her. In the twentieth century romantic interest in Nell and her favourable influence on Charles II reached new heights, and a portrait of her was given to the Hospital. Her name was listed in the Great Hall among the benefactors of the Royal Hospital. The creation and perpetuation of the legend is part of the history of the Hospital, but in the end there is no supporting evidence and it is just a nice story.

ABOVE: *Illustration of Charles II and Nell Gwynne with Chelsea Pensioners from the 1908 programme.*

VIII

Marching On

OPPOSITE: *Andrew Festing's portrait, painted in 1999, of HM Queen Elizabeth II. Two Chelsea Pensioners in the scarlet coat and tricorne hat worn today on ceremonial occasions stand guard at the back, in front of the portrait of Charles II and his family.*

ABOVE: *The Chelsea Pensioners take part each year in the Remembrance Day service at the Cenotaph in Whitehall.*

PREVIOUS PAGE: *March Past of the Chelsea Pensioners at the celebrations for HM Queen Elizabeth The Queen Mother's 100th birthday that took place on Horseguards' Parade in the year 2000. The painting is by Julian Barrow.*

THE CHELSEA PENSIONERS are familiar figures in the streets around the Royal Hospital. In their scarlet coats and black tricornes, wearing medals that are indicative of service to Queen and Country, they are part of ceremonial London. They are important symbols of loyalty, fortitude and the power of tradition. Notable and particularly poignant is their presence at the annual Remembrance Day service at the Cenotaph. The previous evening, at the Festival of Remembrance, twelve of their number who are representative of conflicts of the twentieth century march in slow time down the steps of the Royal Albert Hall to the appreciative clapping of the audience. On these two occasions they are in the company of young men and women of the present-day Armed Forces.

Since the foundation of the Royal Hospital over three hundred years ago ceremonies have evolved that reflect its origins, its values and its royal connections. In the year 2000 the Chelsea Pensioners took part in HM Queen Elizabeth The Queen Mother's 100th Birthday celebrations and two years later in the Services Parade for HM The Queen's Golden Jubilee. Some traditions have disappeared – the Pensioners no longer fire joyous volleys on the birthday of the reigning sovereign – but the main celebration in the calendar is still the Founder's Day parade.

Other ceremonies have emerged, most happening in the run-up to Christmas. In November, in the Great Hall, a vast pudding mixture is stirred by In-Pensioners and staff and then divided into individual portions for each resident; in early December samples of English cheeses are presented to the Royal Hospital by the Dairy Council. Since 1950 these events have been augmented by the presentation to all In-Pensioners of a Christmas cake and a bottle of ale by the Returned and Service League of Australia, in memory of the strong links that have existed for countless years between the two countries. The Chapel is decorated for Christmas and a Carol Service is held in which Pensioners, staff and their families participate.

With generous financial support from Mr Ronald Gerard OBE, a keen benefactor of the Royal Hospital, a magnificent mace was designed and made. In the year of the Queen's Golden Jubilee it was presented by Her Majesty to the Royal Hospital during a ceremony in the gardens of Buckingham Palace. The Sovereign's Mace – a very tangible

FOUNDER'S DAY

ABOVE: *Oak leaf worn on a Pensioner's scarlet coat on Oak Apple Day, as Founder's Day is also called.*

RIGHT: *Part of the Latin lettering on the frieze of the loggia describing the foundation of the Royal Hospital.*

BELOW: *The statue of Charles II in Figure Court decorated with branches of oak.*

SINCE 1692, AND THE ARRIVAL of the first Pensioners at the Royal Hospital, Founder's Day has been celebrated with much ritual, on 29th May or on a day close to that date. This was the birthday of Charles II and also the date of his restoration as king. Escaping from Cromwell's Parliamentary forces after the Battle of Worcester in 1651, Charles hid in the branches of the Boscobel Oak and, in memory of the assistance rendered by the English oak to the monarchy, Chelsea Pensioners and their guests traditionally sport sprigs of oak leaves. The Pensioners are reviewed – sometimes by a member of the Royal Family – and shout three cheers for 'Our pious founder' and for the reigning monarch. Each year a report of this occasion appears in *The Tricorne*, a magazine by and for In-Pensioners and staff. In 2001 the editor, Regimental Sergeant Eric Skentelbery, wrote:

> Princess Alexandra – accompanied by the Governor, General Sir Jeremy Mackenzie, and the Lieutenant-Governor, Major-General Jonathan Hall – took the salute from the dais beneath the statue of Charles II, wreathed for the occasion in the traditional branches of oak. Then came the March Past to the tune of 'The Boys of the Old Brigade', two Companies from the right and two Companies from the left: – it is not as easy as it may sound to those of us in the latter two Companies who have to salute with the left hand; in

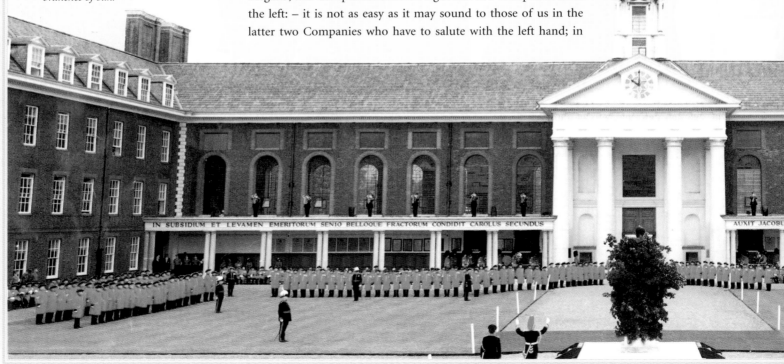

LEFT: *Oak Apple Day 1915. In front of the foliage-wrapped statue stand, from left to right, the Lieutenant-Governor, Major-General Charles Crutchley, the Governor, General the Hon. Sir Neville Lyttelton, and the Adjutant, Major H. Ricardo.*

BELOW: *Inspection of the 'Sitters' by General the Hon. Sir Neville Lyttelton* PC GCB *and Major-General G. J. Farmar* CB CMG, *the Lieutenant-Governor, in 1931.*

fact quite the reverse, that right hand needs to be really fastened down.

The setting for this scene – full of colour and military sound – is Figure Court and the magnificent buildings designed by Wren. Behind the 'Sitters', those Pensioners who are not able to march, is the Latin inscription in the frieze of the loggia IN SUBSIDIUM ET LEVAMEN EMERITORUM SENIO BELLOQUE FRACTORUM CONDIDIT CAROLUS SECUNDUS AUXIT JACOBUS SECUNDUS PERFECERE GULIELMUS ET MARIA REX ET REGINA ANNO DOMINI MDCXCII ('For the Succour and Relief of Veterans Broken by Age and War Founded by Charles the Second Enlarged by James the Second Completed by William and Mary King and Queen in the Year of Our Lord 1692').

ABOVE: *The Mace, donated by Ronald Gerard OBE, was designed by Lieutenant-Colonel Charles Webb and Aubrey Bowden and made by Master Goldsmith Norman Bassant (pictured above) with his son John; Richard Price was responsible for the chased decoration.*

ABOVE RIGHT: *The Sovereign's Mace. The bowl has decoration of oak leaves and acorns associated with Charles II and is surmounted by the St Edward's Crown.*

RIGHT: *HM The Queen, with the Lieutenant-Governor, at Buckingham Palace, at the presentation of the Mace to the Hospital in July 2002.*

FAR RIGHT: *The Sovereign's Mace Bearer, Sergeant-Major Desmond Loat.*

RIGHT: *The woolsack on which the Mace rests in the Museum was donated by The Worshipful Company of Woolmen. Embroidered crests were commissioned from the Royal School of Needlework by The Worshipful Company of Broderers.*

BELOW: *The woolsack is covered with scarlet material similar to that of the Pensioners' coats.*

Secretary

'THIS PLACE IS A BIT LIKE GILBERT AND Sullivan meets Trollope,' explains Michael Legge CB CMG. The observation is prompted not so much by the way in which the Royal Hospital operates but by the splendid uniform that has recently been contrived for the current Secretary – with a Civil Service rather than a military background – to don on ceremonial occasions. There is something about life in the Royal Hospital that makes this description ring true. There are, indeed, the gorgeous uniforms that could come out of a Gilbert and Sullivan operetta. But are there also the deep-laid intrigues, petty jealousies and financial dealings that distinguish the darker moments of Trollope's Barchester novels.

The Secretary of the Royal Hospital held – traditionally – a very important post because he was responsible for paying all Army pensions, not only those of the In-Pensioners. The job changed and in the 1880s the post of Secretary was combined with that of Lieutenant-Governor. Now the jobs are split again. Both Secretary and Lieutenant-Governor report directly to the Governor, with the Secretary being responsible for 'money, staff, buildings and grounds'.

Asked to define the key role of the Secretary now, Legge says, to 'negotiate and control the annual budget (70% of which goes on the wages of the staff) and to maintain and improve 'the splendid set of

Grade I listed buildings'. An additional, specific, task is to develop a plan for the improvement of the Long Wards in the Wren ranges and for the building of the new Infirmary. And this will be tricky. 'We want substantially to improve the quality of the accommodation, but we don't want to do this by halving the number of Pensioners the Royal Hospital can accommodate. This could reduce our income and affect the viability of the whole place.' But then, as he says with a reassuring smile, it is the Secretary's job to make sure that the financial consequences of change are anticipated and that the Royal Hospital continues to do its job into the fifth century of its existence.

symbol of the monarchy's links and involvement with its old soldiers – is now among the Hospital's most precious possessions and is on public display in the Museum.

The management of the Royal Hospital has developed over the years in a somewhat idiosyncratic manner. Indeed, it is something of an anomaly since the Royal Hospital is a public institution but it is not publicly owned or managed. The Board of Commissioners is answerable to itself only, for the Board – and its individual Commissioners – are, legally, the owners of the Hospital and its assets.

Today there is a Board of eighteen Commissioners. Eight hold their appointments by virtue of their office (three government ministers, three serving officers or government officials, and the Governor and Lieutenant-Governor). The other ten 'Specially Appointed' Commissioners are distinguished people selected because of their experience and expertise in areas relevant to the Royal Hospital's work. The Board meets quarterly in the Council Chamber.

The internal administration of the Hospital has always been organized on semi-military lines, with a Governor and other officers. The Governor is supported by the Lieutenant-Governor and the Secretary, and nine heads of departments. Senior staff mainly served in the Army at one time or were employed as civil servants. Originally there were eight companies of In-Pensioners, then six and now there are five, each under the care of a Captain of Invalids. A company has a Company Sergeant-Major and a complement of NCOs drawn from the In-Pensioners to assist in its running.

RIGHT: *The Royal Hospital contingent, led by the Adjutant and Captains of Invalids, march down the Mall in the Golden Jubilee celebrations of 4th June 2002.*

'Up until 1981 the Royal Hospital was part of the Ministry of Defence budget, but now its running costs are met through a Grant-in-Aid,' the Secretary explains. 'The starting point for each annual budget is what you got last year but this is hardly acceptable since each year the Hospital's budget is being "squeezed" by inflation. So, achieving increases in funding is clearly essential. Demonstrating a need to improve access for the disabled can earn an "up-lift" in funding, for instance, and the MoD pay for improvements to the Hospital buildings.'

In the year 2002/3 the Royal Hospital received £8.5 million in Grant-in-Aid. In addition the Hospital receives money from a number of other sources, including donations and legacies, and income from events held in the grounds – including the Chelsea Flower Show organized by the Royal Horticultural Society – and from investments and property. This is all paid into the Army Prize and Legacy Fund (AP&L), which currently makes a contribution of about £1 million a year towards expenditure that could not properly be charged to public funds. Thus, in that particular year, the Royal Hospital operated at a cost of around £9.5 million, which is not a huge sum when its considerable out-goings are taken into account: the accommodation and care of about 350 Pensioners, the salaries of nearly 250 staff and the maintenance – to the highest standards – of a vast stock of historic buildings and sixty-six acres of historic landscape.

The Pensioners' dress has changed little since the nineteenth century. The scarlet coat is worn at ceremonies including the Governor's Parades and on other appropriate occasions such as when Pensioners travel beyond a one-mile radius of the Hospital. The badge of rank worn on the coat depends on whether the Pensioner was discharged from the Regular Army in the rank of sergeant or above. If so, he displays the badge of that

ABOVE: *The Chelsea Flower Show, organized by the Royal Horticultural Society, has taken place on the South Grounds every year since 1913.*

LEFT: *A Pensioner takes his camera to the Flower Show, mingling with the crowds.*

rank; if not, no badge is worn unless he has volunteered to perform a Royal Hospital duty, in which case he wears the Hospital rank badge appropriate to that duty: edging of gold braid to pocket flaps and the top of cuffs indicates that he holds the Royal Hospital rank of sergeant or above.

The 'working cap' bears the badge of the wearer's old regiment or corps and may only be worn within the Hospital grounds. Outside, a Pensioner is seen wearing a shako bearing the letters 'RH' or the tricorne if attending a ceremony where a member of the Royal Family is present.

Pensioners, nowadays, are somewhat older than they used to be when they enter the Royal Hospital and tend to have more disabilities. Their average age is over eighty and the average number of years spent as a resident is seven. There is little doubt that living at the Royal Hospital helps significantly to prolong life.

The type of man who decides to become an In-Pensioner has changed. Traditionally, the Army had been the life of most of the Pensioners and they had probably had only a few years as civilians before entering the Royal Hospital (the age of entry after the Second World War was as low as fifty-five). But now most of the In-Pensioners have had longer civilian than military lives; indeed, many have had successful careers since leaving the Army. This means that not only do the In-Pensioners have more diverse experiences and interests but their financial circumstances are more robust.

The Pensioners still have to surrender their military pensions and war disability payments when they enter the Royal Hospital. Though regarded as just, this used to be somewhat tough as it left them with very little money for the pleasures of old age. But now most residents have an income beyond their Old Age Pension (that all retain) in the form of pensions from their civilian employment.

The increased prosperity, and the experience of the modern comforts available in most homes, is having a profound influence on the Royal Hospital. Quite simply, if the Royal Hospital is to continue to fulfil its historic function, it has to meet standards of accommodation that will attract sufficient numbers to make its operation viable. It has to change.

A development plan prepared in 2002 by Donald Insall Associates suggested the form the changes might take. The most controversial of these was what the architects described as 'improving the environment and living conditions of the In-Pensioners housed in Wren's Long Wards'.

The Long Wards have already been altered, between 1953 and 1957 and again in the 1990s, finishing in 1996. Three of the original berths have been reconfigured to form two larger units and ceilings, which were taken out in the 1920s, have been given to each berth. The work was carried out with great skill. The oak joinery was left untouched (every third door was simply sealed) and all looks much as it did in Wren's day. But, to provide Pensioners with the standard of accommodation that complies with current

ABOVE: *In June Mendoza's painting, Frank Chambers* BEM *is in the centre of the group. On his birthday in 1943 he led his squad a yard or two too far – to right on the German lines. He spent the rest of the war as a prisoner. His companions are Jack Rogerson, Sam Weekes, Michael McClean* BEM *and Joe Britton.*

legislation – and that most take for granted – an additional series of changes to the berths was proposed. Some berths, it was suggested, should be further modified to provide more bathing and toilet facilities. The problems were recognized as complex – not least because of the integration of a large amount of plumbing within the historic fabric of the building. There would also be the impact on the Hospital of taking a considerable number of berths out of commission.

Improved communications were seen as an important issue. An internet café is now available for In-Pensioners, but their need for access to external communications will continue to grow. Individual telephone and computer facilities were therefore included in the development scheme.

ABOVE: *Master Woodcarver Hugh Wedderburn at work on the royal coat of arms for the Parade Chair.*

RIGHT: *The Parade Chair, for use on public occasions, was presented to HM The Queen by the Royal Hospital to commemorate her Golden Jubilee.*

The provision of accommodation for In-Pensioners that reflects current expectations of comfort and convenience was clearly the central goal of the proposals. But other suggested changes were almost as radical. For example, the Royal Hospital is well aware that in due course accommodation for women soldiers will need to be provided. This has not been done before and, even though numbers are likely to be small, it would have a marked effect on the ethos of the Royal Hospital. It can only happen when suitable accommodation is available, to the same standard as that provided for the men.

The Royal Hospital has only ever provided for ex-soldiers. If demand decreased – although, given the expectation that there will be greater numbers eligible to become In-Pensioners over the next thirty years or so, this is unlikely to happen – then access by those who have been in other Services might need to be considered. Unlike the entry of women (which has never been officially prohibited), this would require a change in the Royal Hospital's constitution.

Also proposed in the development plan is the use of the Soane stable block (currently occupied by the Surveyor of Works and his department) as a new museum and visitor centre linked with the adjoining National Army Museum, and the creation of a new Infirmary.

The construction of a new Infirmary will involve the demolition of the functional but far from handsome early 1960s Infirmary that fronts on to Chelsea Bridge Road and its replacement with a new building. The work will have to be carefully phased. Before demolition can take place the north-east wing – rebuilt for the second time in the 1950s and presently containing additional Long Wards – will be converted into a temporary forty-bed Infirmary so that medical care can continue. The Royal Hospital recognizes that the project will represent a great opportunity. Not only must it fit with the adjacent buildings by Wren and Soane but also, because of its very public location on the edge of the Royal Hospital site, the new Infirmary must make a positive contribution to the area.

On the evening of 26th February 2003 I met five of the men in the Club to talk about how the Royal Hospital works. It is, after all, for them that the institution was created and it is for them that it is maintained. They are the people who matter.

The Club is a pleasing and convivial room, created within the former Servants' Hall in the north-west wing and retaining much of its 1680s panelling. A bar stretches along one side with the remainder of the space occupied by neat rows of tables and chairs. Next to the Club, to the east (in the former Officers' Hall), is a billiard room and, beyond that (in the former Housekeeper's Hall), is a room dedicated to a large television that sits in one corner. The bar, like the other rooms, has walls covered with photographs, paintings and memorabilia. This wing is very much the social heart of the Hospital.

The first of my companions was Sergeant Ralph Dickinson, aged seventy-eight, a former member of the Parachute Regiment and sergeant in the Durham Light Infantry, now a Ward Sergeant at the Royal Hospital (which he entered in 2000). He is a man of quiet authority and sound common sense. Sergeant Edward 'Buck' Taylor, aged eighty-two, of the Royal Signals, after being evacuated from Dunkirk was attached to Ist Commando Brigade and landed on Sword Beach on D-Day, fighting across north-west Europe into Germany. Buck Taylor has a very individual view of affairs and a great sense of fun and irony. His record shows that he was a soldier of great initiative – he tricked his guard and escaped after being captured in France in 1940 – and is not a man to give officers and the authorities an easy ride. He entered the Royal Hospital in 2001. Corporal John Jones makes the third of this trio of close friends. Because of links through the Parachute Regiment he knew Ralph Dickinson well before joining the Royal Hospital in 2002. John Jones also has a great, youthful sense of fun and he, too, was at the cutting edge of military service during the war. In 1943 he transferred from the King's Shropshire

Light Infantry into the Parachute Regiment and in 1944 was dropped at Arnhem where he was, eventually, taken prisoner.

Private William Germanes was born in Hackney, north-east London, in 1914. From 1941 he served with the Loyal Regiment (North Lancashire) and, from 1943, with the Royal Artillery. As a gunner with a Light Anti-aircraft Regiment he took part in the D-Day landings of 6th June 1944 and ended the war on the outskirts of Hamburg. He entered the Royal Hospital in 1999. The last of the group was Sergeant Geoffrey Payne, who in 1948 joined the Nottinghamshire Yeomanry and in later, civilian life was Mayor of Hinckley & Bosworth. He joined the Royal Hospital in 1999.

The first question I asked the veterans was how they came to be in the Royal Hospital. Ralph Dickinson explained the current terms of eligibility: an Army Service Pension for at least eleven and a half years' service or an Army Disability Pension; aged sixty-five or over; no dependants; and of good character. I asked what 'good character' actually means. How bad would an ex-soldier's character have to be before he was refused entry? No one was absolutely sure but concluded that it would have to be pretty bad – near diabolical – for entry to be refused.

Bill Germanes explained what happened to him, as a general example. He married a Dutch girl soon after the war and they 'enjoyed twenty-six years of happy married life together'. Then, alone, he decided to apply for the Royal Hospital. 'You come in for a trial period – four days – to see if they like you and if you like them.' All thought this a good system. As Ralph Dickinson pointed out, 'You know pretty quickly if the life's going to suit you, you know within a month if you will settle down'.

I asked, since all of them had enjoyed long careers in civilian life after leaving the Army, if they found the military regime of the Hospital – uniforms and parades, rank and authority – difficult to adjust to. All agreed this raised no real problems – and not just because all men who have served in the Army have had to evolve a knack for living in a military environment. Ralph Dickinson explained that the Royal Hospital makes few demands of its residents. 'You don't have to do anything if you don't want to, and the facilities and privacy are way above anything we knew in the Army.' But, of course, not everyone is happy. 'Life here is what you make it,' mused Ralph Dickinson. 'With 350 men in here you will always find a few who are bad tempered and resentful; some are pretty chippy and feel hard done by and some have difficult memories to deal with. These can resurface as you get older.'

'What about the obligations of communal life of the Hospital and the requirement to wear a uniform? Do you feel institutionalized,' I asked. These questions made them

LEFT: *Chelsea Pensioners out and about in the King's Road.*

all smile broadly and it was quite clear no one felt in the least institutionalized. As John Jones made plain, the great advantage of the Hospital is that it encourages you to lead an active life. 'You get another lease of life. You get ten extra years of life being here.'

The reason for this was easy to explain: good companionship, very good healthcare and – perhaps most important – a sense of purpose, usefulness and responsibility. All Pensioners who are physically able are encouraged to take a role in running the Royal Hospital and its facilities (such as being a Ward NCO, librarian or guide for visitors), which can earn them a little extra money. Alternatively, they can get involved in useful and beneficial activities such as gardening or in various crafts. Whichever they do, it keeps them positive, focused and young in spirit.

Sitting with my five companions, the benefits of this regime were obvious. They all retain an enthusiasm, humour, interest, delight in company – a sparkle of youth – that it would be difficult, if not impossible, to find in any other institution housing so many old men. Certainly Buck Taylor – with his mischievous smile, anarchic comments and wry humour – must be much the same man he was sixty years ago when he outwitted his German captors and then cheerfully diced with death in Normandy. As for the uniform, none saw this as a problem. John Jones said that, because of it, 'I've never met so many women! It opens doors and frequently you are not allowed to buy a drink in a pub. It can get a bit embarrassing'. Ralph Dickinson recalls that he nearly caused a riot when he went home to Durham wearing his scarlet coat. 'Women came up to me and asked if I was a real Chelsea Pensioner. They were excited, said they had never seen one!'

What about the future, what about change? Should women be admitted? This question produced a moment of silence. All realized that, in a world of equal opportunities where women have all the rights and responsibilities of men, women who have served in the Army, risked their lives for their regiment and country, deserve the same benefits as male soldiers. Indeed, they acknowledged that there is a legal as well as moral obligation to admit women. But old habits die hard and the majority of these old soldiers – youthful as they seem – are not quite of the modern world and prefer to stay true to the principles of an earlier age. One voice seems to speak for all: 'Women – let them have equality – but not in here'. As John Jones felt obliged to add, more in hope perhaps than in horror, 'Things happen you know – regardless of age'.

As if to banish the disturbing – even tantalizing – prospect of women holding court in the Club, the existing benefits of life in the Royal Hospital are reeled off. Frequent outings, good food, 'free barber and laundry,' enthuses Bill Germanes. 'Yes, you get well looked after,' added Buck Taylor, 'you even get cremated free of charge.' Bill Germanes reflected for a moment. 'I have no regrets – not for a single day.' Nor did Geoff Payne. He has had, perhaps, a wider experience of life than most In-Pensioners but does not find the institution in any way inhibiting. It fact he remains amazed to have been admitted as a resident. 'I didn't realize I had a right to be here. I think a lot of old soldiers who have spent years in civilian life are in the same position. I assumed you had to be very special to deserve a place in the Royal Hospital, to have a George Medal or something.'

The Chelsea Pensioners have served, some of them with recognized distinction, in different regiments and corps of the British Army and in different times and places. The character of the British soldier is one of courage, endurance, skill and adaptability. This is the blend of qualities that helps to make the British Army one of the most admired in the world.

In acknowledgement of their contribution to society, the Chelsea Pensioners of the future deserve to retire to a place that will provide them with relief and comfort in their last decades. Change will inevitably come to the Royal Hospital, and it must be carefully and sensitively handled to ensure that the need for stability of current Pensioners is met while at the same time the requirements of the next generation are taken into account. The Royal Hospital is well equipped to handle such a challenge since it has always recognized the importance of the individual and the value of maintaining standards and traditions.

Perhaps the last word should come from the family of an In-Pensioner. 'My father was a Chelsea Pensioner for the last four and a half years of his life. He loved the place, where he found camaraderie, outstanding medical care and the chance to live his final years free from the stresses and strains of everyday life.' Praise indeed.

THE ROYAL HOSPITAL FROM THE AIR

Chelsea Bridge

South Grounds

Ranelagh Gardens

Figure Court

Roman Catholic
Chapel and Library

Light Horse Court

Soane's Secretary's Block

College (Infirmary) Court

Infirmary

West Road

East Road

Soane's Stable Block

Burton's Court

Chapel

Great Hall

In-Pensioners' Club

Octagon Porch

READING LIST

The key book on the Royal Hospital is C. G. T. Dean's *The Royal Hospital Chelsea*. Published in 1950, it was the result of much detailed research undertaken by Dean when he was one of the Hospital's Captains of Invalids. It remains the authoritative work on the institution. David Ascoli's *A Village in Chelsea*, published in 1974, is also a useful book although expressing some distinctly odd views – presumably current at the time – about Soane's contributions to the Royal Hospital.

For detailed information about the evolution of the Hospital, its design and construction, the *Survey of London: Chelsea (part 4)*, vol. XI, of 1927, and *The Wren Society*, vol. XIX, of 1942, are essential.

Very good books, throwing light on key characters or aspects of the Royal Hospital are: Christopher Clay's *Public Finance and Private Wealth: the Career of Sir Stephen Fox, 1627–1716*, of 1978; Kerry Downes's *Christopher Wren*, of 1971; Phillis Cunnington and Catherine Lucas's *Charity Costumes*, of 1978. See also Margaret Richardson's 'Soane at Chelsea', *The Chelsea Society Report*, of 1992.

For accounts of veterans, Pensioners, soldiers and relevant military actions see: Philip Ziegler's *Soldiers: Fighting Men's Lives, 1901–2001*, of 2001; Martin Snow and Robin Ollington's *Before they Fade: Reminiscences of a Soldier's Life by Today's Chelsea Pensioners*, of 2002; Michael Mann's *The Veterans*, of 1997; Matthew Stephens's *Hannah Snell: The Secret Life of a Female Marine, 1723–1792*, of 1997; Percy A. Scholes's *The Great Doctor Burney*, 2 vols, of 1948; William Murrell Lummis's *Honour the Light Brigade*, of 1973; R. H. Murray's *The History of the VIIIth King's Royal Irish Hussars, 1693–1927*, of 1927; John Bierman and Colin Smith's *Alamein: War without Hate*, of 2002; and James Lucas's *War in the Desert: the Eighth Army at El Alamein*, of 1982.

Of older books dealing with the Royal Hospital, the Pensioners and military life, the most important and informative are: R. Walker's *The Female Soldier, or the Surprising Life and Adventures of Hannah Snell*, of 1750; Christopher Wren's *Parentalia; or, Memoirs of the Family of the Wrens*, of 1750; W. H. Pyne's *The Costume of Great Britain*, of 1805; Thomas Faulkner's *An Historical and Topographical Description of Chelsea and its Environs*, of 1810; John Teesdale's *Military Torture*, of 1835; and a number of books by a former Chaplain of the Royal Hospital named G. R. Gleig including *Chelsea Pensioners*, of 1829, *Chelsea Hospital and its Traditions*, of 1839, and *Veterans of Chelsea Hospital*, of 1842.

LIST OF SUBSCRIBERS

Ms Heather Addison
Mr Denis Barnham
Mr Henry Biddle
Mr Charles Biddle
Carole J. Blackshaw, Lady
    Mayoress of London
Karsten Borch
Peter Burke CI
Mr and Mrs Simon Camamile
Mrs Pamela Chattey
Jos Coad
Richard and Rosanne Corben
Sir Michael Craig-Cooper CBE
    TD DL
Lieutenant Colonel Denis
    Daly
Edward A. Fitzgerald
Ian Frazer
Susan Grinling
Norman Gunby
Major General and Mrs
    Jonathan Hall
R. W. Harris
Christopher Hodsoll
Pat Horn
Richard Hunting
I/P 205 5th Royal Inniskilling
    Dragoon Guard
Peter and Sara Kendall
Mrs Doris Lee
Michael and Linda Legge
A/Sgt W. Lumsden
Sid Lunn
General Sir Jeremy Mackenzie
R/Sgt Bob Martin
Victor G. Massingham
Colin McCourt
Henry McHale
Stuart W. Mitchell
Mr and Mrs Edward Nelson
Michael G Parr MBE
Geoffrey Payne
Christopher J. R. Pope TD

Master F. C. M. Prickett
Christine and David Robinson
Veronica Smith
Spink and Son Ltd
The Institute of Cancer
    Research, Chelsea
Phoebus N. Theologites
I/P 307, Tony Tremarco
Duggie Waterhouse
Ben Oliver Whittington
Mr F. E. B Witts
Mr Lucio Zagari

**Belgravia Traders
Association Members**
Ayrton Wylie
Bainboroughs
Baker & Spice
Belgravia Gallery
Ben de Lisi
Best Gapp & Cassells
Boisdale
Boyd
Cluttons
Crichton
De Vroomen
DTZ Residential
Duncan Lawrie Ltd
E. B. Meyrowitz
Eaton Square Garage
Ebury Wine Bar
Elizabeth Street Veterinary
    Clinic
Erickson Beamon
Friend & Falcke
George Trollope
H & M Interiors
Henry Stokes Stationers
Hutchinson Mainprice
Jeroboams
John D Wood & Co
Joss Graham
La Campagnola

Les Senteurs
Lime Tree Hotel
Mimmo d'Ischia
NatWest Bank Plc
Oliveto
Oliviers & Co
Philip Treacy
Poîlane
Serena le Maistre & Associates
SMA Consultants Ltd
The Chocolate Society
The Exchange
Tomtom Cigars
Tophams Belgravia
Waldens Chymist
Vantis WS
Woodhams
Worldly Goods
Young England

**Additional sponsors for the
Elizabeth Street Carnival,
19th June 2003**
AnonymousDonation.org
Anya Hindmarch
Blackbird Productions
Brechin Management Ltd
British Airways
De Vere Group Plc
Detta Phillips
Duke of Wellington
English Heritage Hospitality
FPD Savills
Friars Inn
Gaming Corporation Plc
Golden Bottle Trust
Goya Restaurant
Grosvenor
H J Heinz Company Ltd
Hilton International
Holloway White Allom
Hotel Ambassadeur Concorde
    Juan Les Pins

Hugo & The Huguenots
Hunters & Frankau
J O Hambro Investment
    Management
James Connell Esq
Jimmy Choo
Kensington House Hotel
London Area Amusements
Marriott Harbour Beach
    Hotel & Spa
McKay Securities Group
Monte's
Mosimann's
Number Eleven Cadogan
    Gardens
Pestana Hotels & Resorts
Real Events Europe Ltd
Royal Sun & Alliance
Savoy Resort – Madeira
Shepherd Neame
Sofitel St James's Hotel
The Apsley Health Club
The Berkeley
The Cadogan
The Chester Grosvenor
The English Garden School
The Goring
The Halkin
The Lowndes Hotel
The Ritz London
The Sloane Club
Threshers
W. A. Ellis
Wildtracks
Williamson Moore Ltd
Woolworths

INDEX

PICTURE ACKNOWLEDGEMENTS

All illustrations are from the collection of the Royal Hospital Chelsea with the exception of those listed below. The author and publishers are most grateful to these people and institutions for their kind permission to publish.

Cover: background picture Guildhall Library, Corporation of London
Back cover inset: Peter Smith
Front endpapers: Royal Borough of Kensington & Chelsea
Back endpapers: Guildhall Library, Corporation of London
© Julian Barrow, by kind permission of Col. Nigel Gilbert 164/165
Bodleian Library, Oxford 24/25
Bridgeman Art Library, London 60/61, 94, 127 *left*, 131, 132, 134
Coram Foundation, London (photo Bridgeman Art Library) 80
Courtauld Institute of Art, London. Witt Library 70 *top*
© Andrew Festing 167
Guildhall Library, Corporation of London 36, 56, 81, 89, 91
Illustrated London News 147 *right*
Irish Museum of Modern Art, Royal Hospital Kilmainham 20 *top*
© June Mendoza 176
Mobilier National, Paris (photo Giraudon/Bridgeman Art Library) 18
National Army Museum, London 62, 93, 96, 97, 104, 118/119
National Galleries on Merseyside (photo Bridgeman Art Library) 5, 137
National Maritime Museum, Greenwich 145
Pepys Library, Magdalene College, Cambridge 26, 29
Royal Borough of Kensington & Chelsea 39, 72, 83, 84, 86, 87, 88, 99, 100, 101, 133, 148 *top left*
Sir John Soane's Museum, London 102/103, 105, 106, 108 *top*, 110, 112, 113, 115, 116
Topham Picturepoint 158
Victoria & Albert Museum, London (photo Bridgeman Art Library) 121

Photography at the Royal Hospital
Sophie Baker 10, 11, 160
Bridgeman Art Library 14/15, 16, 21 *top*, 23, 34, 78/78, 82, 85, 120, 124, 134, 142/143, 144, 146, 157, 162, 163 *top left*, 167
Julian Calder 12
Edifice Photo Library 70 *bottom*, 139, 174 *left*
Tim Graham 170, 171, 177
Tina Hadley 77
Angelo Hornak 2, 7, 20 *bottom*, 35, 42 *bottom*, 43, 44, 46, 47, 48, 49, 51, 58, 63, 64, 65, 66/67, 68, 73, 95, 123, 127 *right*, 135, 147 *centre*, 159
Peter Smith 17, 32/33, 42 *top*, 45, 76, 126, 168, 174 *right*, 179, 180, 183
Tim Soar 31, 40, 59, 109, 117